CROSS STITCH
SUPERHEROES

MORE THAN 40 PATTERNS

PUNTO DE CRUZ
SUPERHEROES

MÁS DE 40 PATRONES

Welcome!

Welcome to the exciting world of cross-stitch with superheroes! This book is designed to combine the creativity of embroidery with the magic of the most iconic characters from the comic book world. Whether you're a beginner or an expert in the art of cross-stitch, you'll find projects here that will inspire and challenge you.

Cross-stitch is an accessible and rewarding embroidery technique, perfect for capturing the vibrant and dynamic essence of superheroes. This book includes a variety of patterns, from classics like Superman and Wonder Woman to contemporary heroes like Spider-Man and Black Panther. Each design comes with detailed instructions, clear charts, and helpful tips to ensure your project's success.

Superheroes represent values such as courage, justice, and perseverance. As you work on your projects, we hope you find inspiration in their stories and that each stitch brings you closer to your heroes, allowing you to carry a bit of their spirit with you.

Prepare your needle and your most vibrant threads, and dive into this creative adventure. Let the mission begin, and enjoy every stitch as you create heroic works of art in cross-stitch!

¡Bienvenido!

¡Bienvenidos al emocionante universo del punto de cruz con superhéroes! Este libro está diseñado para combinar la creatividad del bordado con la magia de los personajes más icónicos del mundo del cómic. Ya seas un principiante o un experto en el arte del punto de cruz, aquí encontrarás proyectos que te inspirarán y desafiarán.

El punto de cruz es una técnica de bordado accesible y gratificante, perfecta para capturar la esencia vibrante y dinámica de los superhéroes. Este libro incluye una variedad de patrones, desde los clásicos como Superman y Wonder Woman, hasta los contemporáneos como Spider-Man y Black Panther. Cada diseño viene con instrucciones detalladas, gráficos claros y consejos útiles para asegurar que tu proyecto sea un éxito.

Los superhéroes representan valores como el coraje, la justicia y la perseverancia. Mientras trabajas en tus proyectos, esperamos que encuentres inspiración en sus historias y que cada puntada te acerque más a tus héroes, permitiéndote llevar un poco de su espíritu contigo.

Prepara tu aguja y tus hilos más vibrantes y sumérgete en esta aventura creativa. ¡Que comience la misión y disfrutes cada puntada en tu camino para crear obras de arte heroicas en punto de cruz!

Glossary / Glosario

English	**Español**
Design size	Tamaño del diseño
Puntadas	Puntadas
Floss list for crosses	Lista de hilos
Use 2 Strands of thread for cross stitch	Usa 2 hilos de hilo para punto de cruz
Symbol	Simbolo
Number	Número
Name	Nombre

Material to use / Material a utilizar

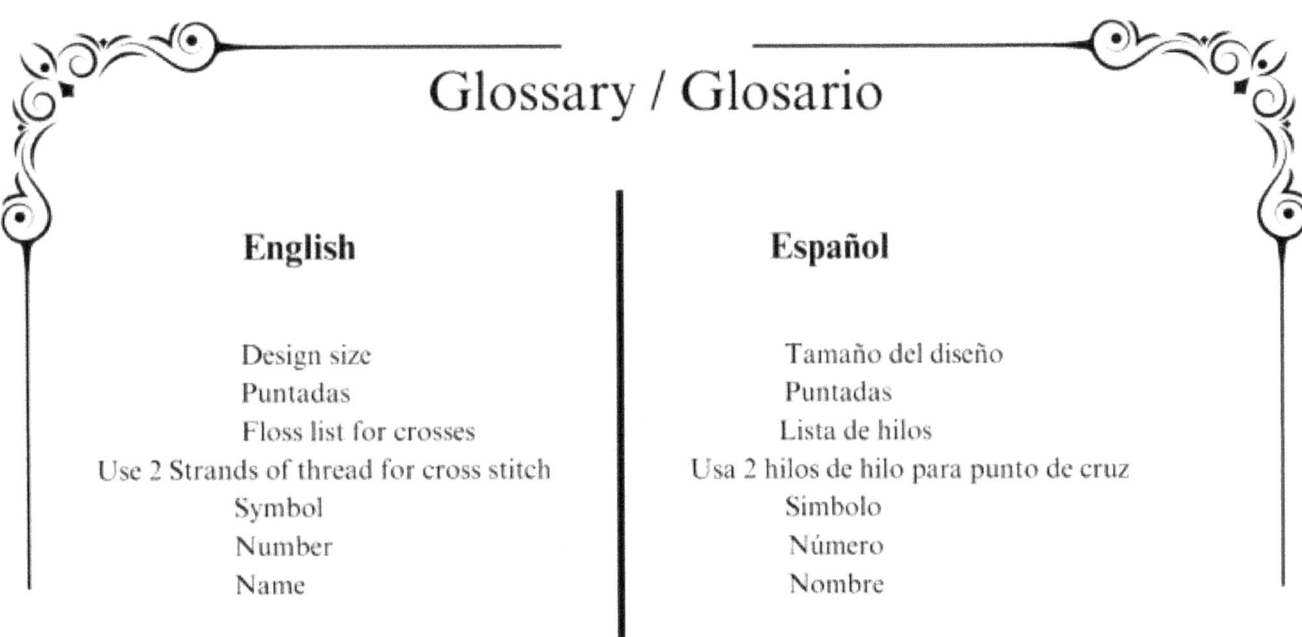

Thread DMC / Hilo DMC

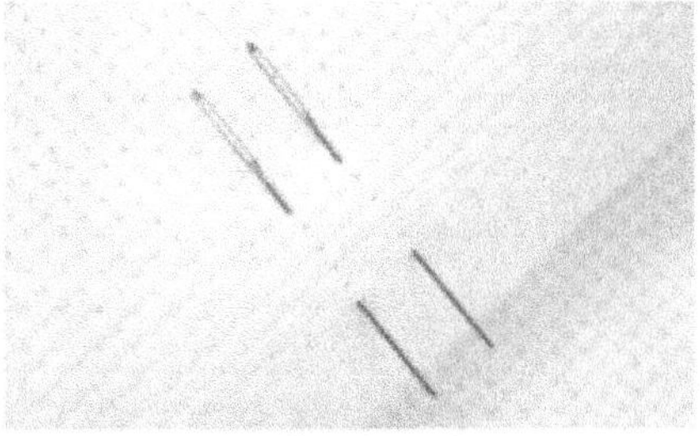

Needles / agujas

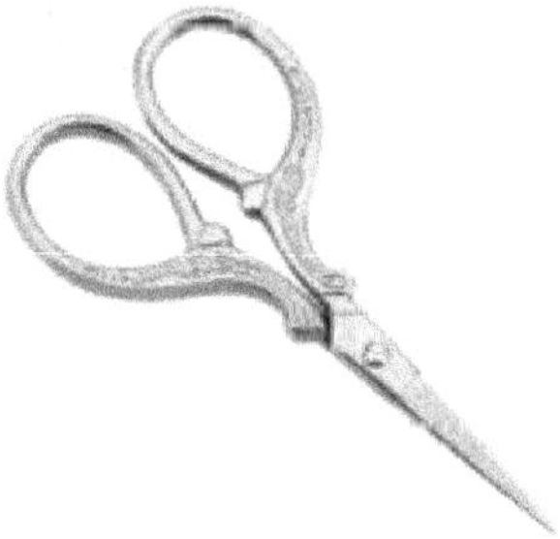

Scissors / Tijeras

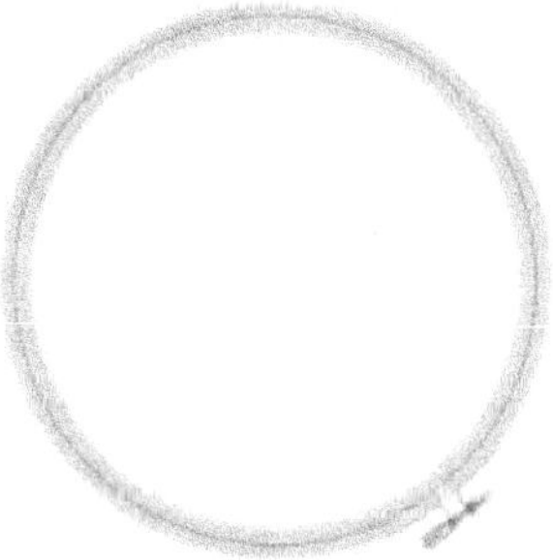

Hoop / Aro

Fabric / Tela

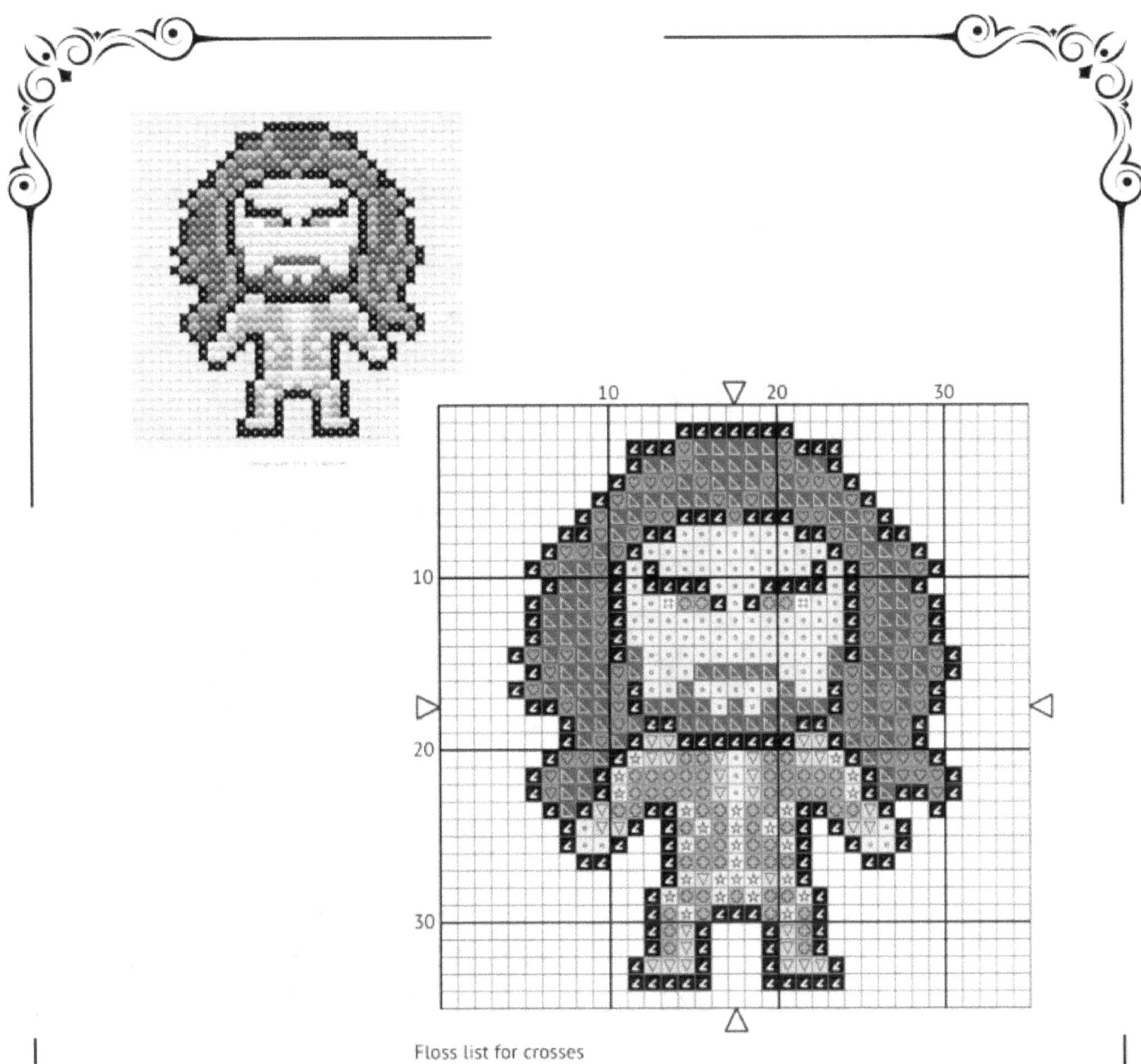

Floss list for crosses

Use 2 strands of thread for cross stitch

N	Symbol		Number	Name	Stitches
1	♯	♯	DMC B5200	Snow White	2
2	☆	☆	DMC 307	Lemon	27
3	◢	◢	DMC 310	Black	174
4	▽	▽	DMC 444	Lemon - Dark	32
5	◺	◺	DMC 610	Drab Brown - Dark	131
6	♡	♡	DMC 841	Beige Brown Light	82
7	○	○	DMC 951	Tawny - Light	102
8	❖	❖	DMC 3846	Bright Turquoise - Light	63

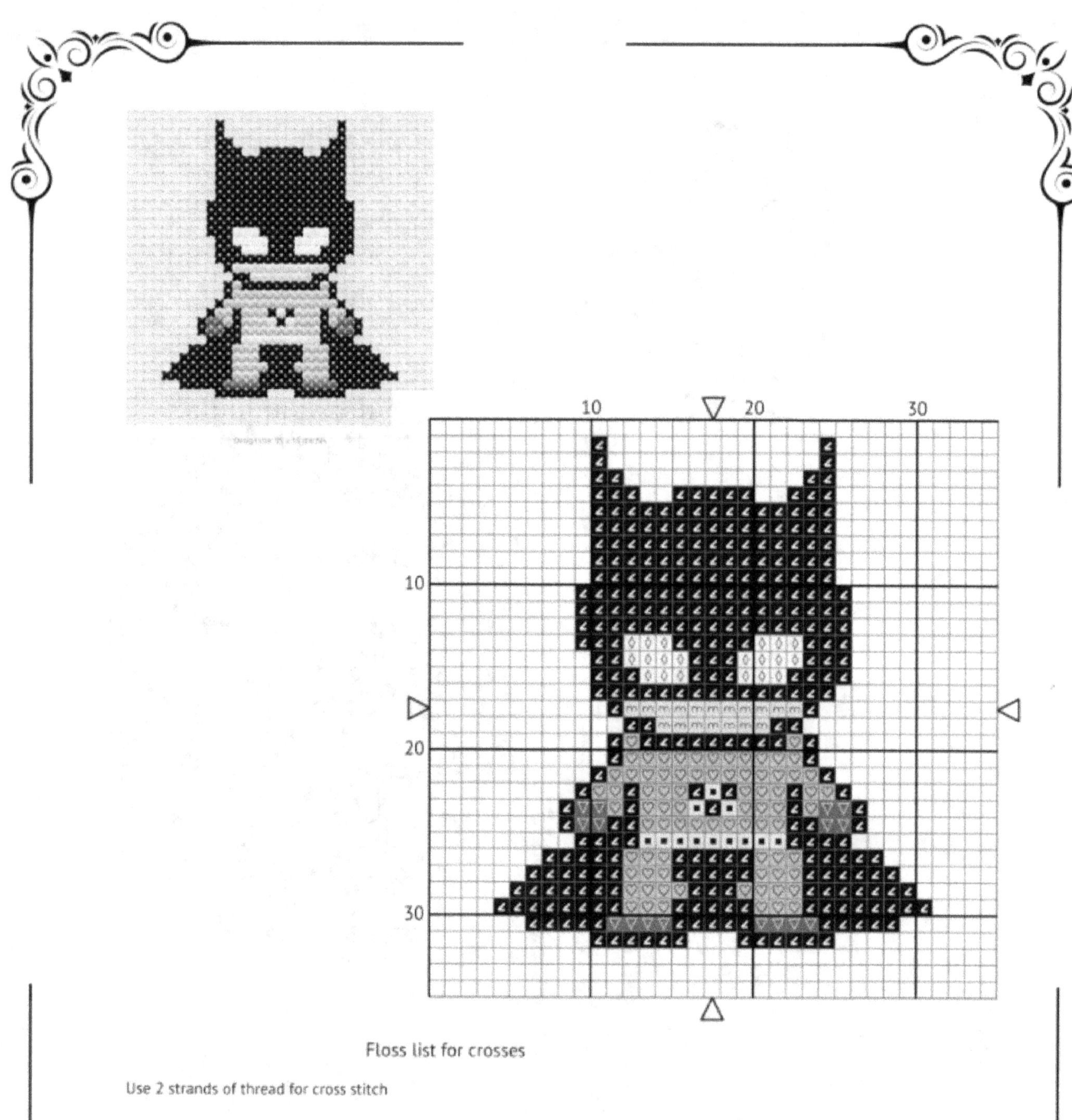

Floss list for crosses

Use 2 strands of thread for cross stitch

N	Symbol		Number	Name	Stitches
1	◇	◇	DMC B5200	Snow White	20
2	■	■	DMC 307	Lemon	12
3	◣	◣	DMC 310	Black	332
4	♡	♡	DMC 928	Gray Green - Very Light	79
5	▽	▽	DMC 3768	Gray Green - Dark	16
6	m	m	DMC 3774	Desert Sand - Very Light	18

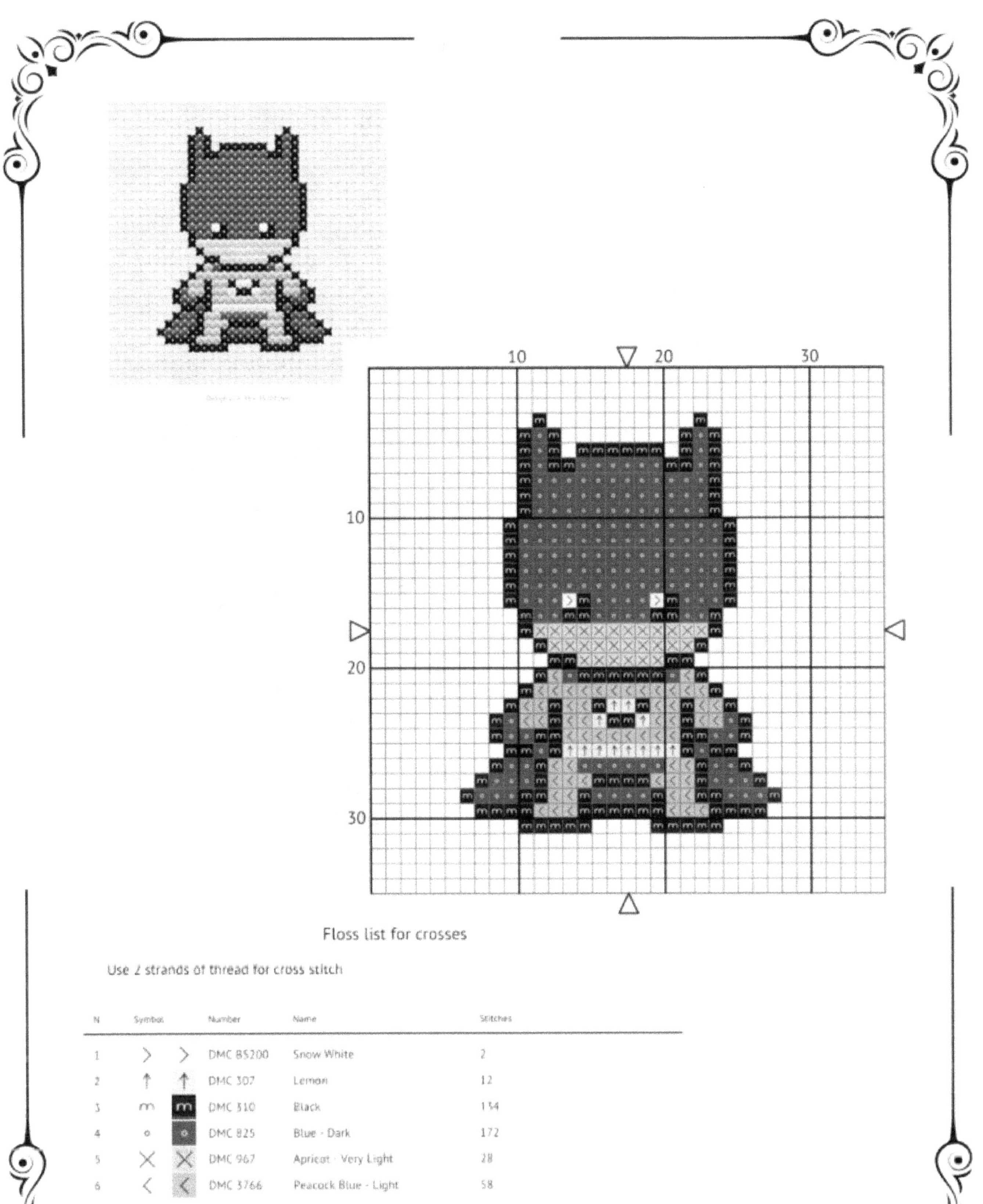

Floss list for crosses

Use 2 strands of thread for cross stitch

N	Symbol		Number	Name	Stitches
1	>	>	DMC B5200	Snow White	2
2	↑	↑	DMC 307	Lemon	12
3	m	m	DMC 310	Black	154
4	o	o	DMC 825	Blue - Dark	172
5	✕	✕	DMC 967	Apricot - Very Light	28
6	<	<	DMC 3766	Peacock Blue - Light	58

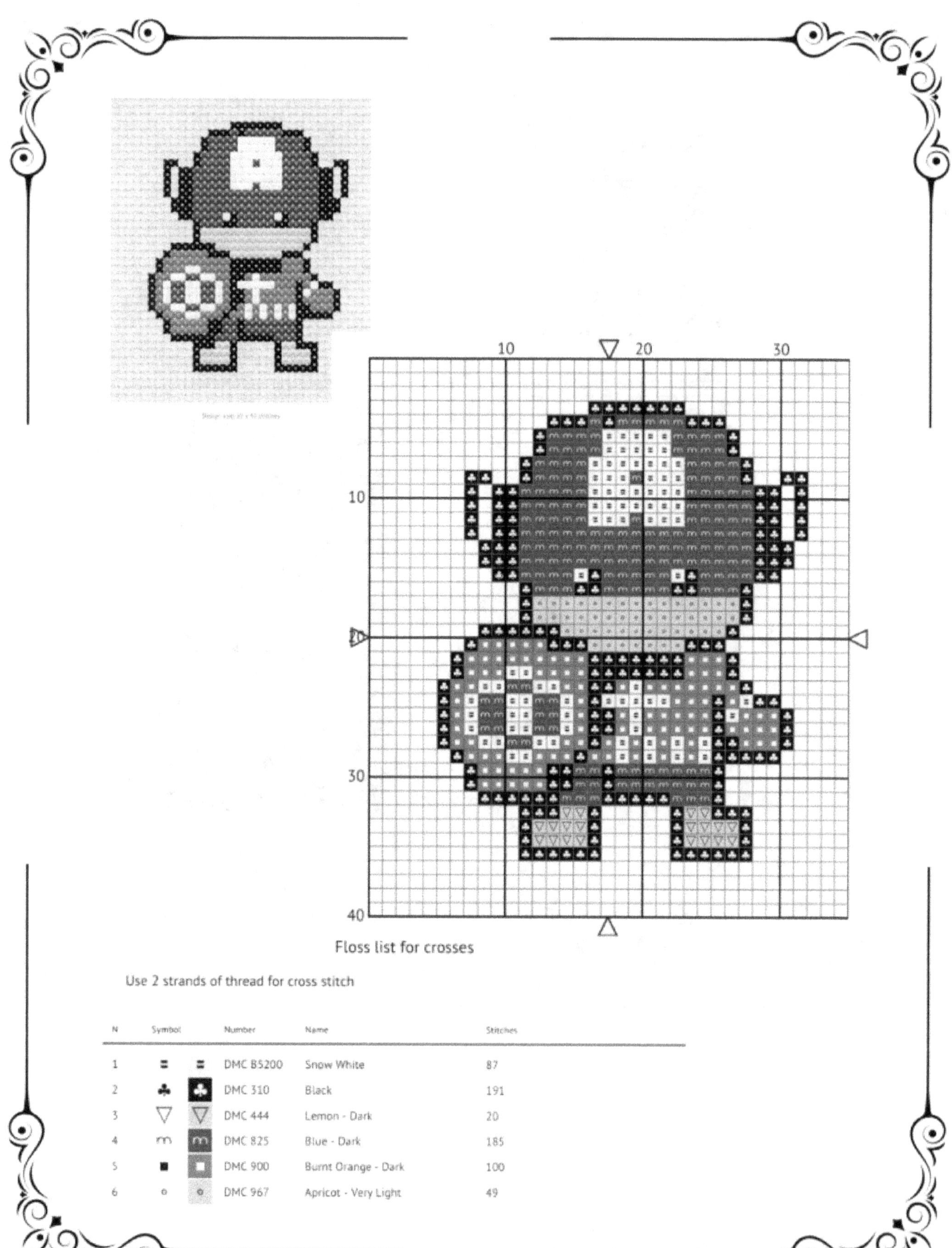

Floss list for crosses

Use 2 strands of thread for cross stitch

N	Symbol		Number	Name	Stitches
1	≡	≡	DMC B5200	Snow White	87
2	♣	♣	DMC 310	Black	191
3	▽	▽	DMC 444	Lemon - Dark	20
4	m	m	DMC 825	Blue - Dark	185
5	■	■	DMC 900	Burnt Orange - Dark	100
6	o	o	DMC 967	Apricot - Very Light	49

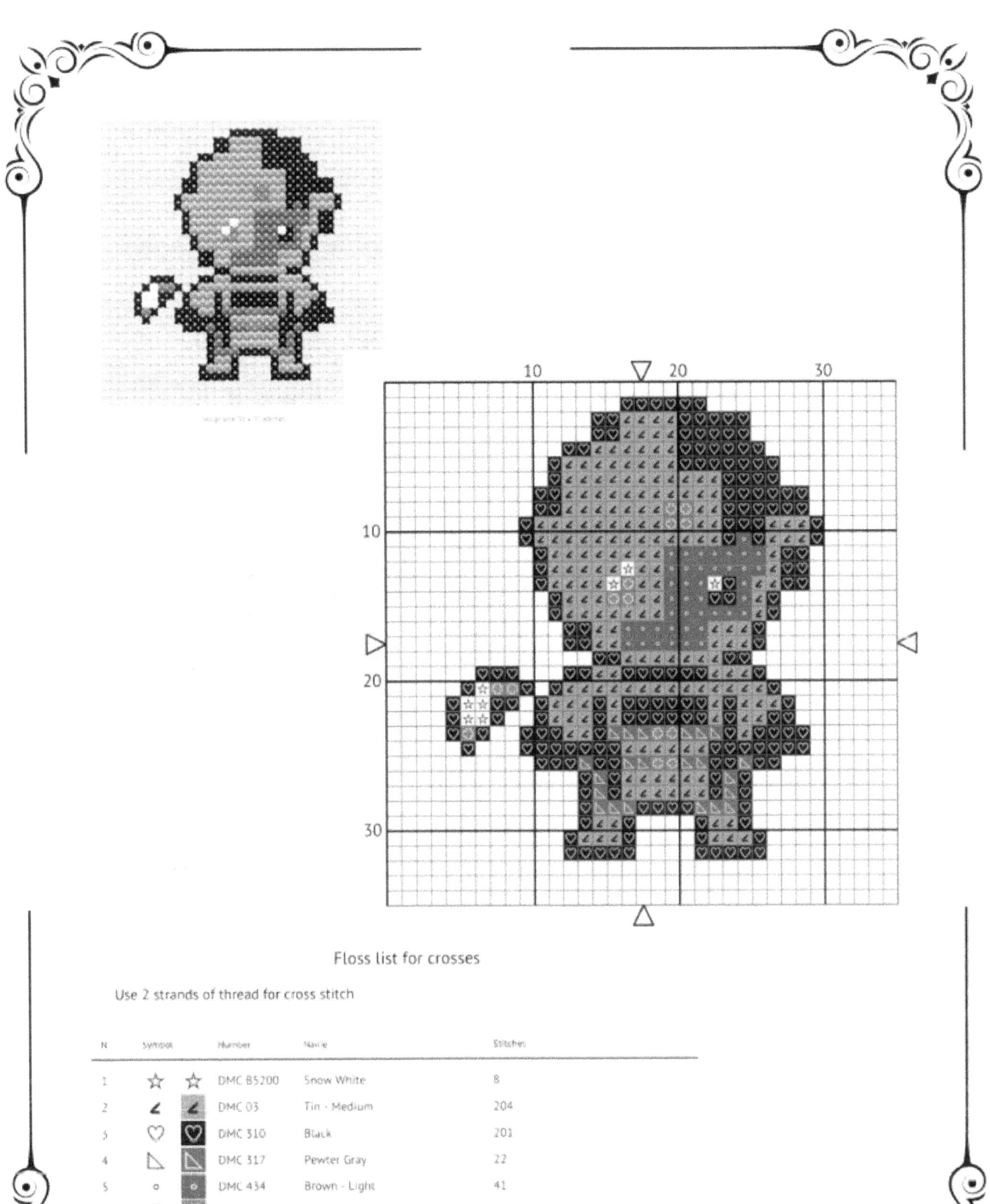

Floss list for crosses

Use 2 strands of thread for cross stitch

N	Symbol		Number	Name	Stitches
1	☆	☆	DMC B5200	Snow White	8
2	◢	◢	DMC 03	Tin - Medium	204
3	♡	♥	DMC 310	Black	201
4	◺	◺	DMC 317	Pewter Gray	22
5	○	◉	DMC 434	Brown - Light	41
6	✜	✜	DMC 900	Burnt Orange - Dark	14

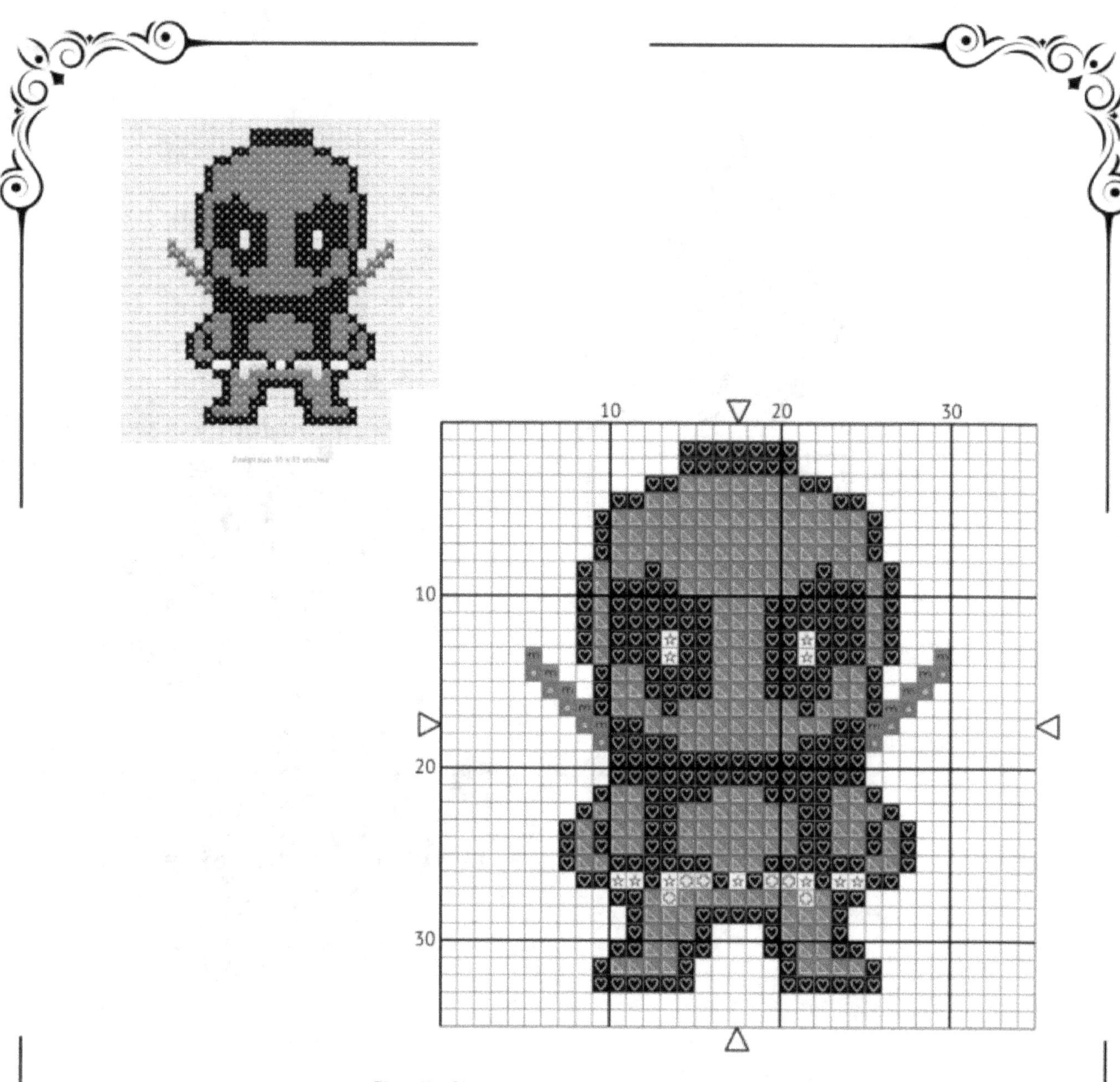

Floss list for crosses

Use 2 strands of thread for cross stitch

N	Symbol		Number	Name	Stitches
1	☆	☆	DMC B5200	Snow White	11
2	✿	✿	DMC 307	Lemon	6
3	♡	♥	DMC 310	Black	253
4	◺	◺	DMC 817	Coral Red - Very Dark	238
5	m	m	DMC 926	Gray Green - Medium	10
6	◦	◦	DMC 3790	Beige Gray - Ultra Dark	10

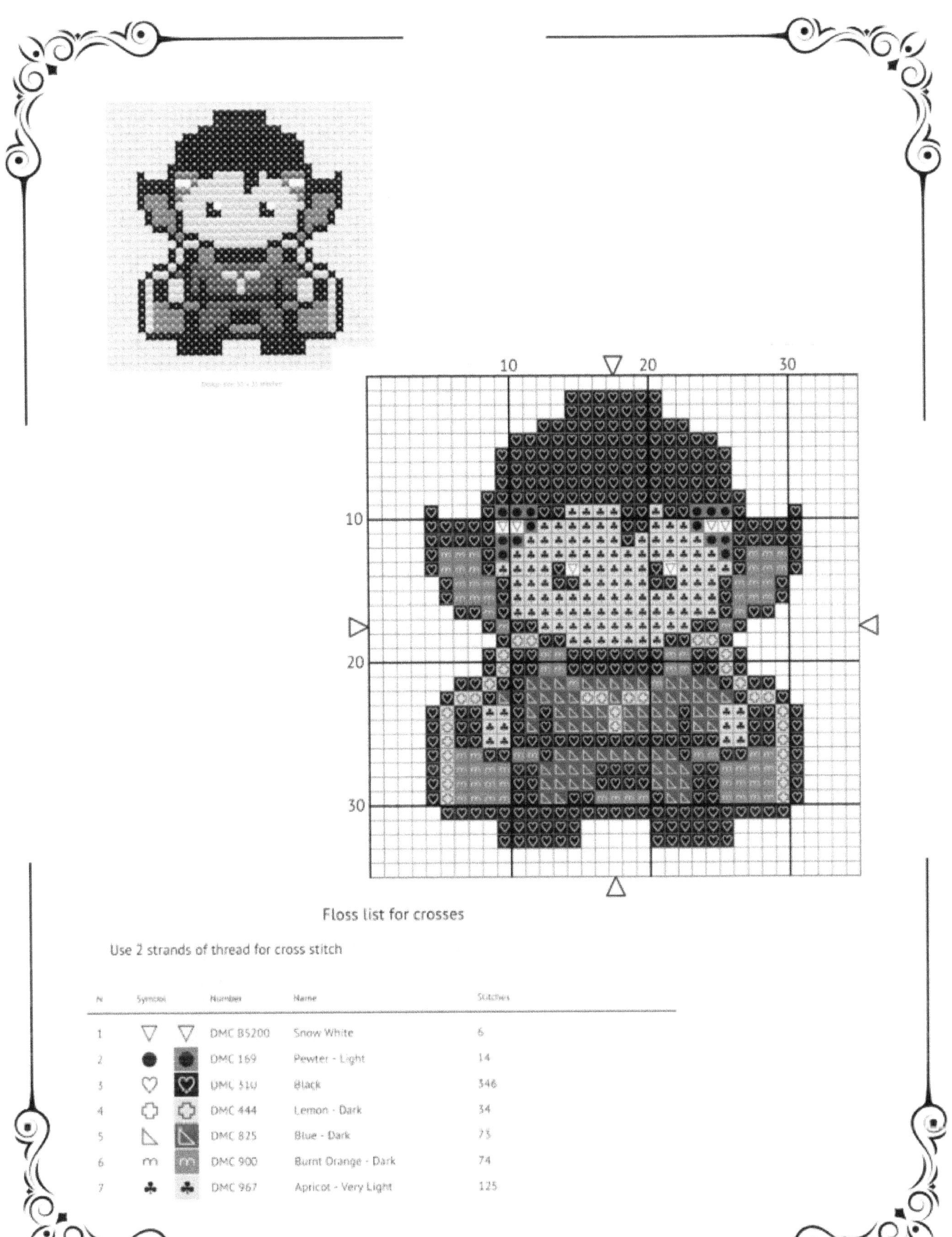

Floss list for crosses

Use 2 strands of thread for cross stitch

N	Symbol	Number	Name	Stitches
1	▽ ▽	DMC B5200	Snow White	6
2	● ●	DMC 169	Pewter - Light	14
3	♡ ♥	DMC 310	Black	346
4	♧ ♧	DMC 444	Lemon - Dark	34
5	◺ ◺	DMC 825	Blue - Dark	73
6	m m	DMC 900	Burnt Orange - Dark	74
7	♣ ♣	DMC 967	Apricot - Very Light	125

I AM
GROOT

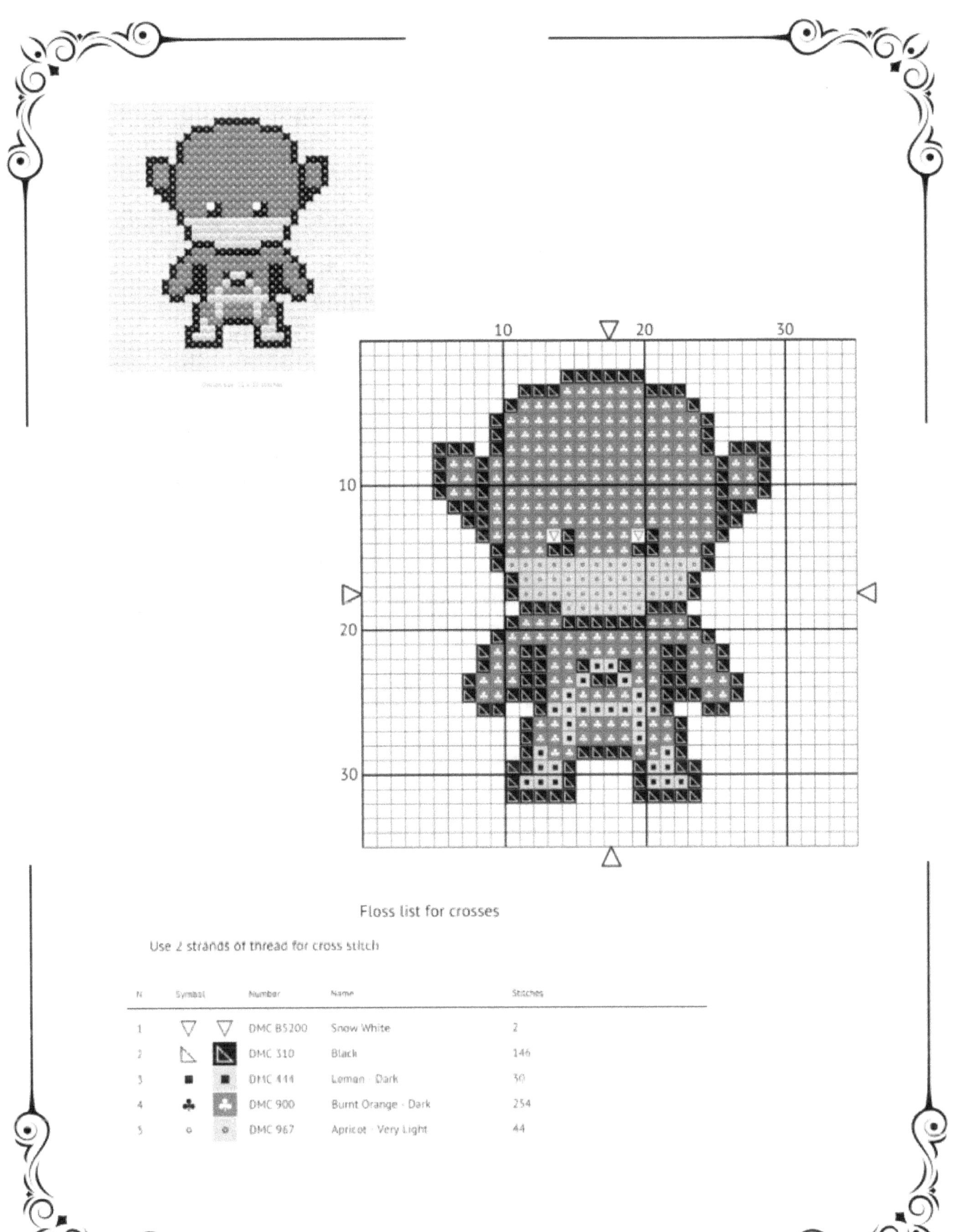

Floss list for crosses

Use 2 strands of thread for cross stitch

N	Symbol		Number	Name	Stitches
1	▽	▽	DMC B5200	Snow White	2
2	◣	◣	DMC 310	Black	146
3	■	■	DMC 444	Lemon - Dark	30
4	♣	♣	DMC 900	Burnt Orange - Dark	254
5	○	○	DMC 967	Apricot - Very Light	44

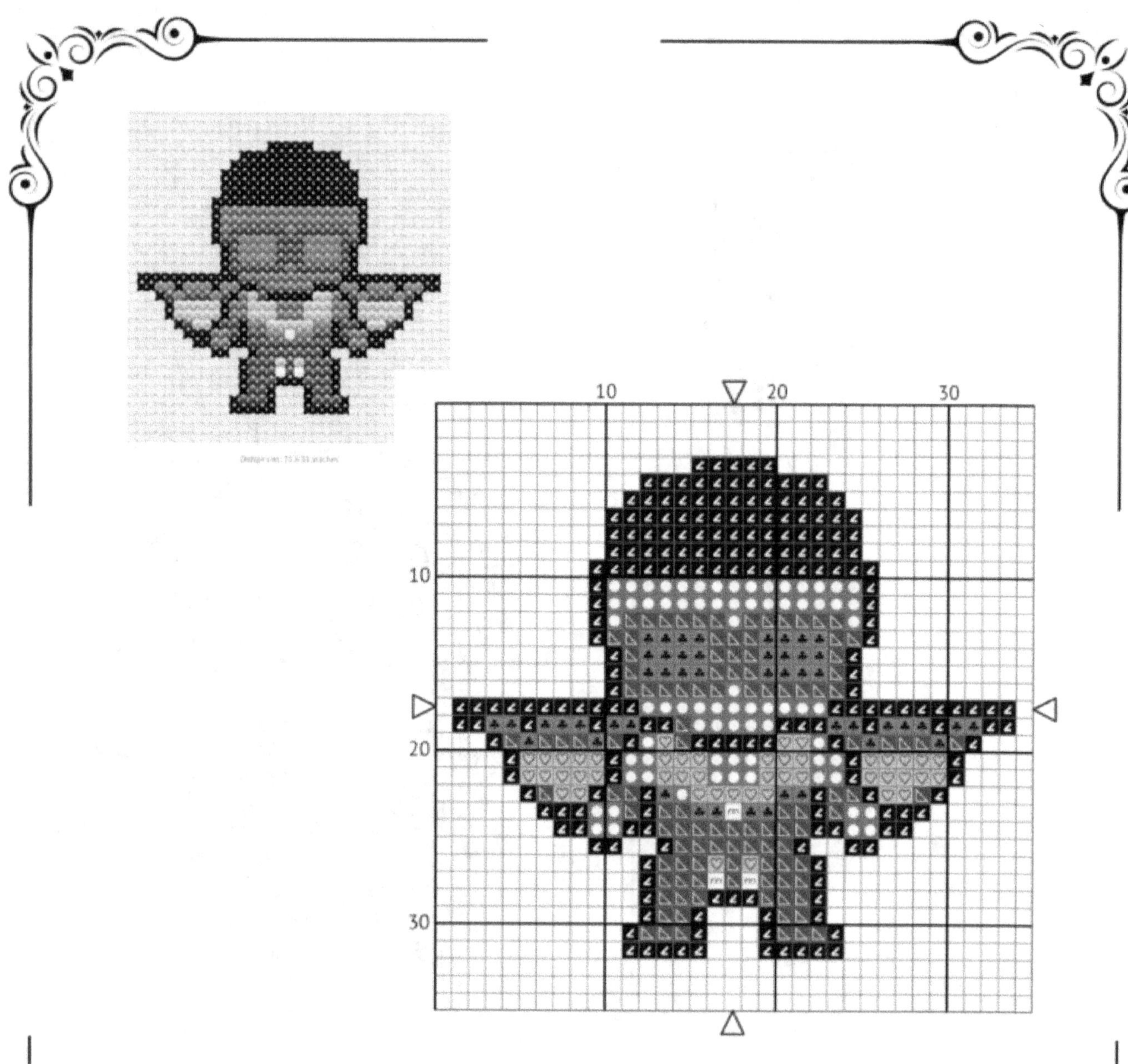

Floss list for crosses

Use 2 strands of thread for cross stitch

N	Symbol		Number	Name	Stitches
1	m	m	DMC B5200	Snow White	3
2	⊿	⊿	DMC 310	Black	212
3	◹	◹	DMC 413	Pewter Gray - Dark	111
4	♡	♡	DMC 928	Gray Green - Very Light	46
5	●	○	DMC 3829	Old Gold - Very Dark	75
6	♣	♣	DMC 3832	Raspberry - Medium	49

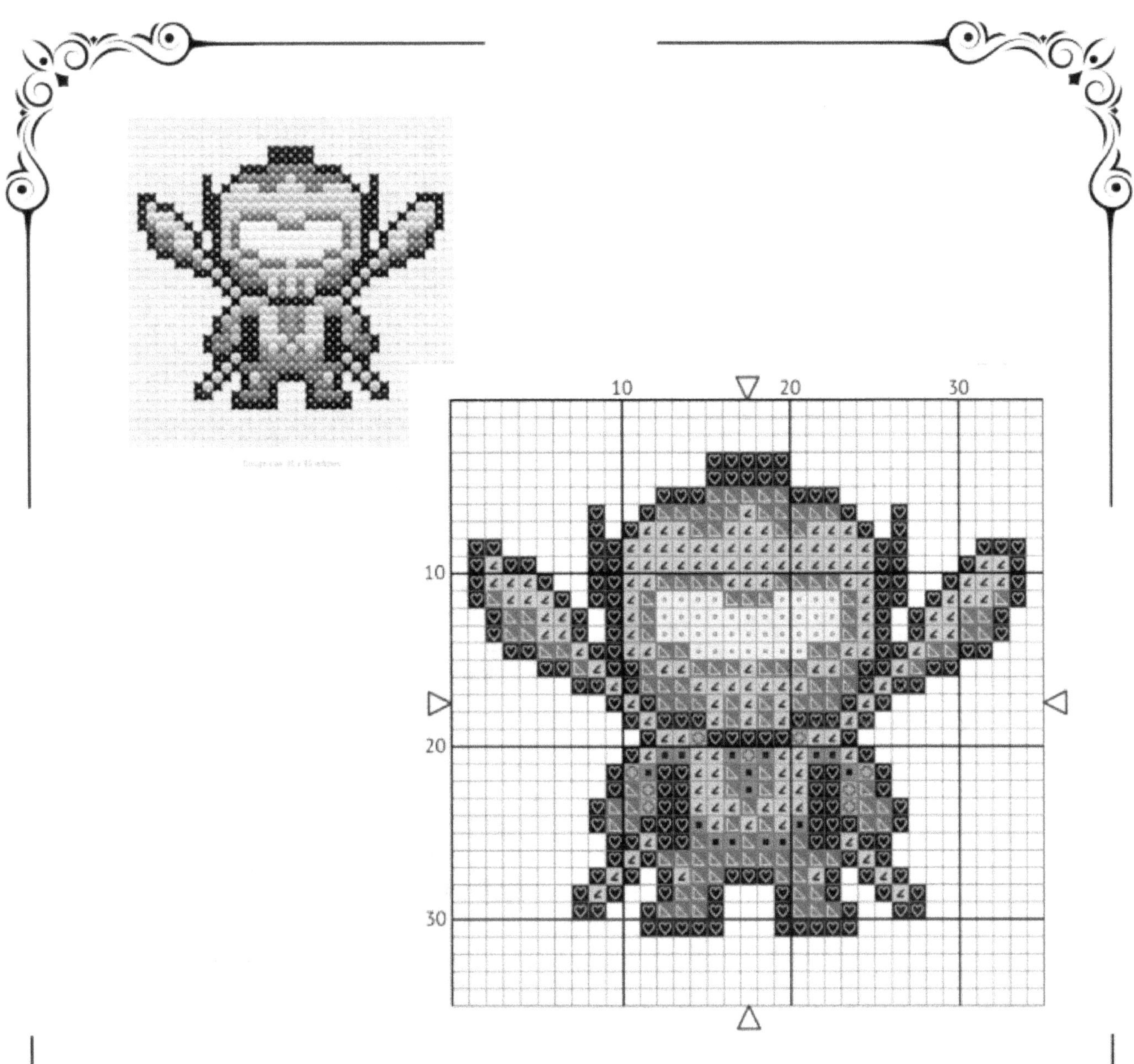

Floss list for crosses

Use 2 strands of thread for cross stitch

M	Symbol		Number	Name	Stitches
1	○	○	DMC 307	Lemon	37
2	♡	♥	DMC 310	Black	186
3	∠	∠	DMC 928	Gray Green - Very Light	145
4	⬡	⬡	DMC 996	Electric Blue - Medium	9
5	◁	◁	DMC 3768	Gray Green - Dark	125
6	■	■	DMC 3832	Raspberry - Medium	16

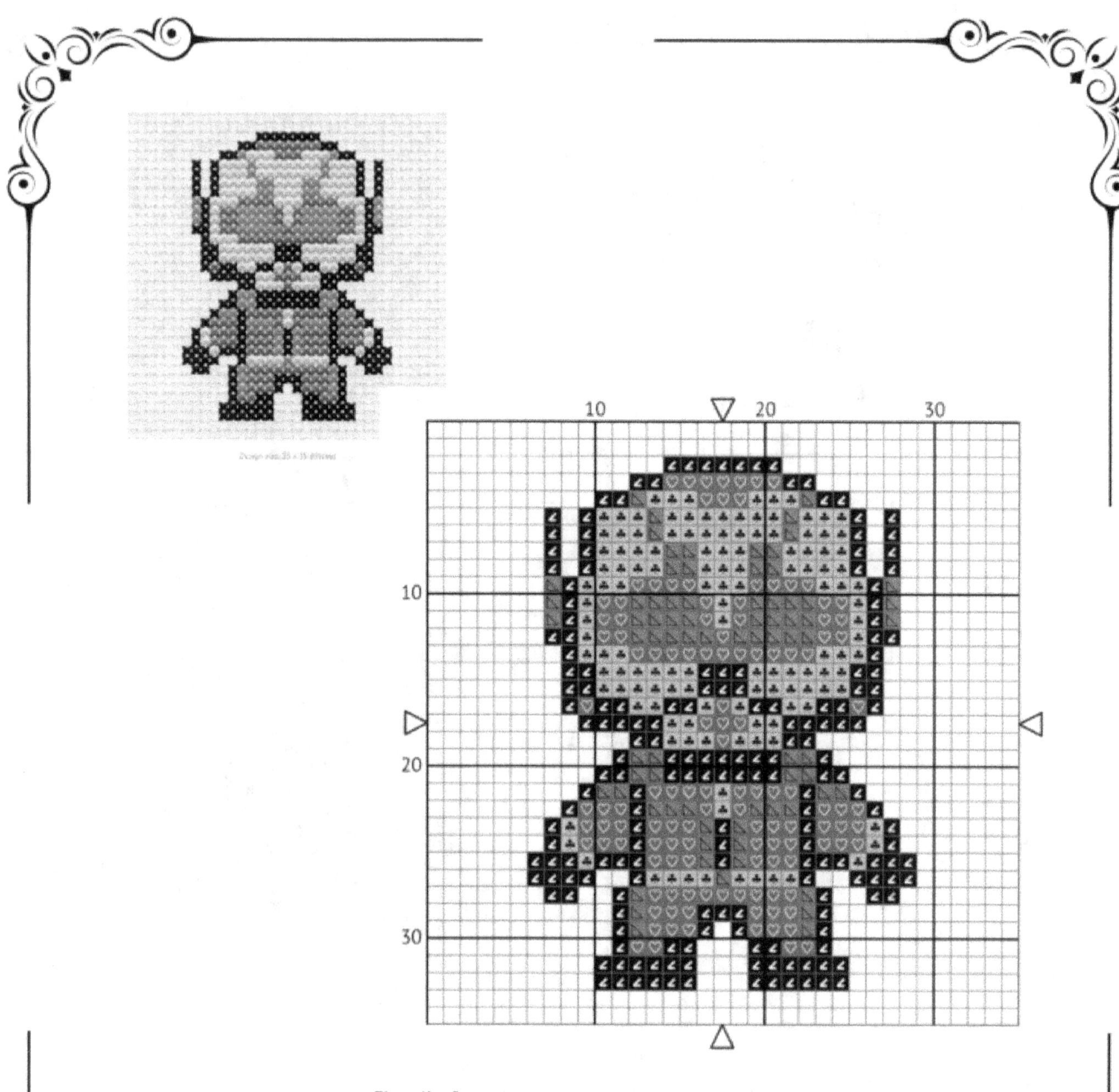

Floss list for crosses

Use 2 strands of thread for cross stitch

N	Symbol		Number	Name	Stitches
1	✎	✎	DMC 310	Black	187
2	♣	♣	DMC 928	Gray Green - Very Light	133
3	♡	♡	DMC 3768	Gray Green - Dark	124
4	◺	◺	DMC 3832	Raspberry - Medium	77

Floss list for crosses

Use 2 strands of thread for cross stitch

N	Symbol		Number	Name	Stitches
1	m	m	DMC B5200	Snow White	2
2	♡	♥	DMC 310	Black	232
3	◺		DMC 911	Emerald Green - Medium	199
4	♣	♣	DMC 3837	Lavender - Ultra Dark	32

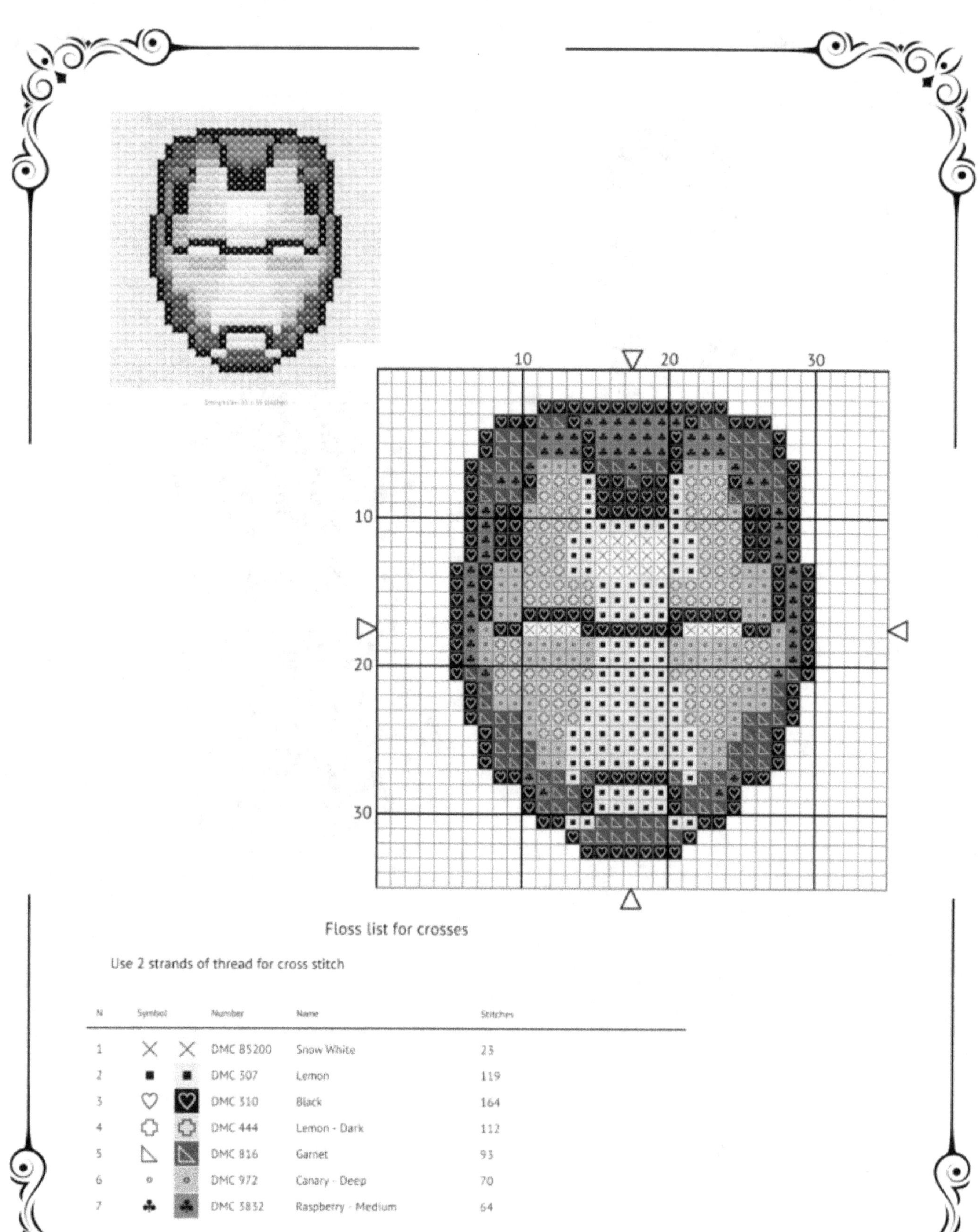

Floss list for crosses

Use 2 strands of thread for cross stitch

N	Symbol		Number	Name	Stitches
1	✕	✕	DMC B5200	Snow White	23
2	■	■	DMC 307	Lemon	119
3	♡	♥	DMC 310	Black	164
4	✿	✿	DMC 444	Lemon - Dark	112
5	◺	◣	DMC 816	Garnet	93
6	∘	∘	DMC 972	Canary - Deep	70
7	♣	♣	DMC 3832	Raspberry - Medium	64

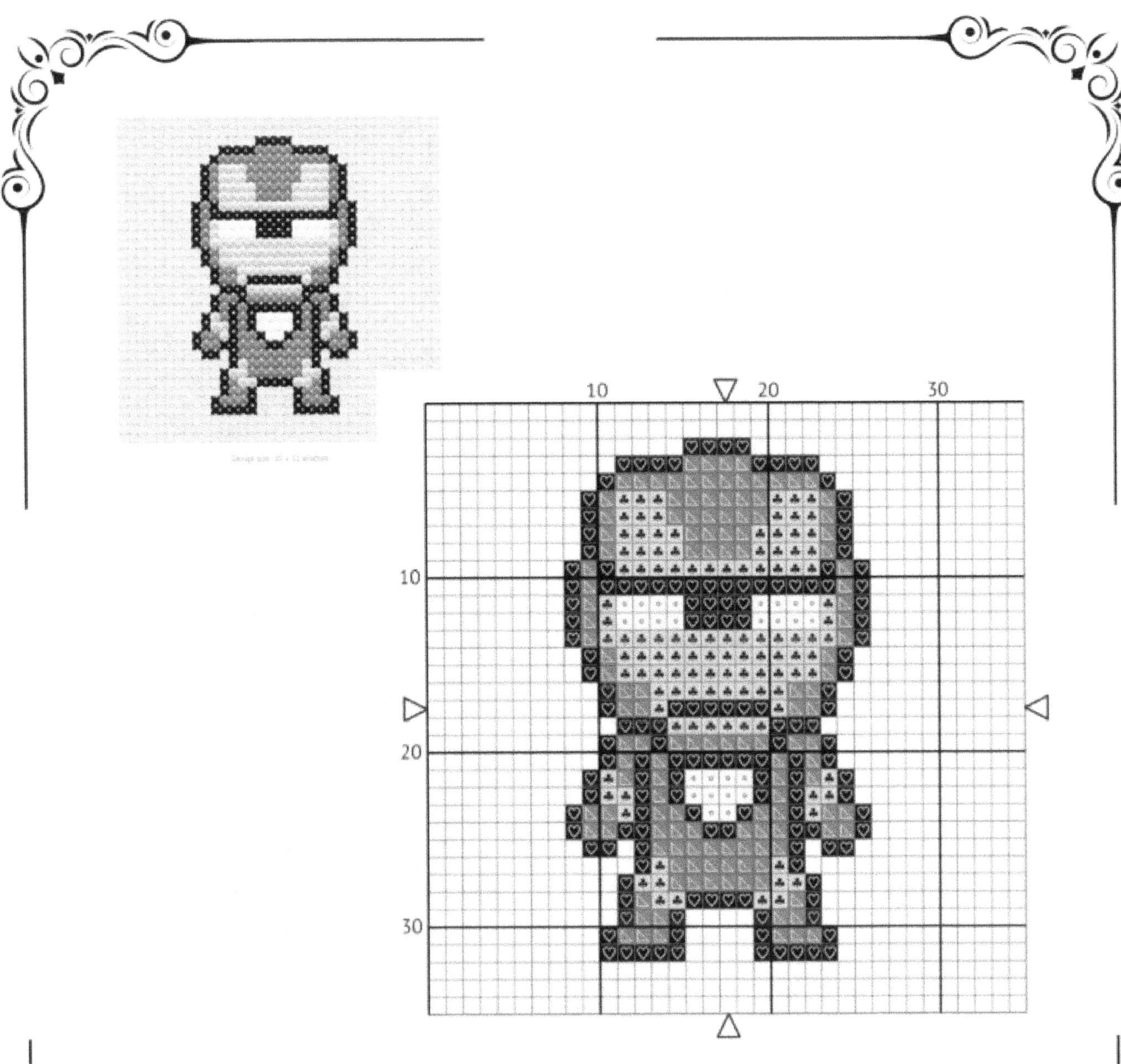

Floss list for crosses

Use 2 strands of thread for cross stitch

N	Symbol		Number	Name	Stitches
1	○	○	DMC B5200	Snow White	26
2	♡	♥	DMC 310	Black	150
3	♣	♣	DMC 444	Lemon - Dark	116
4	◹	◥	DMC 900	Burnt Orange - Dark	136

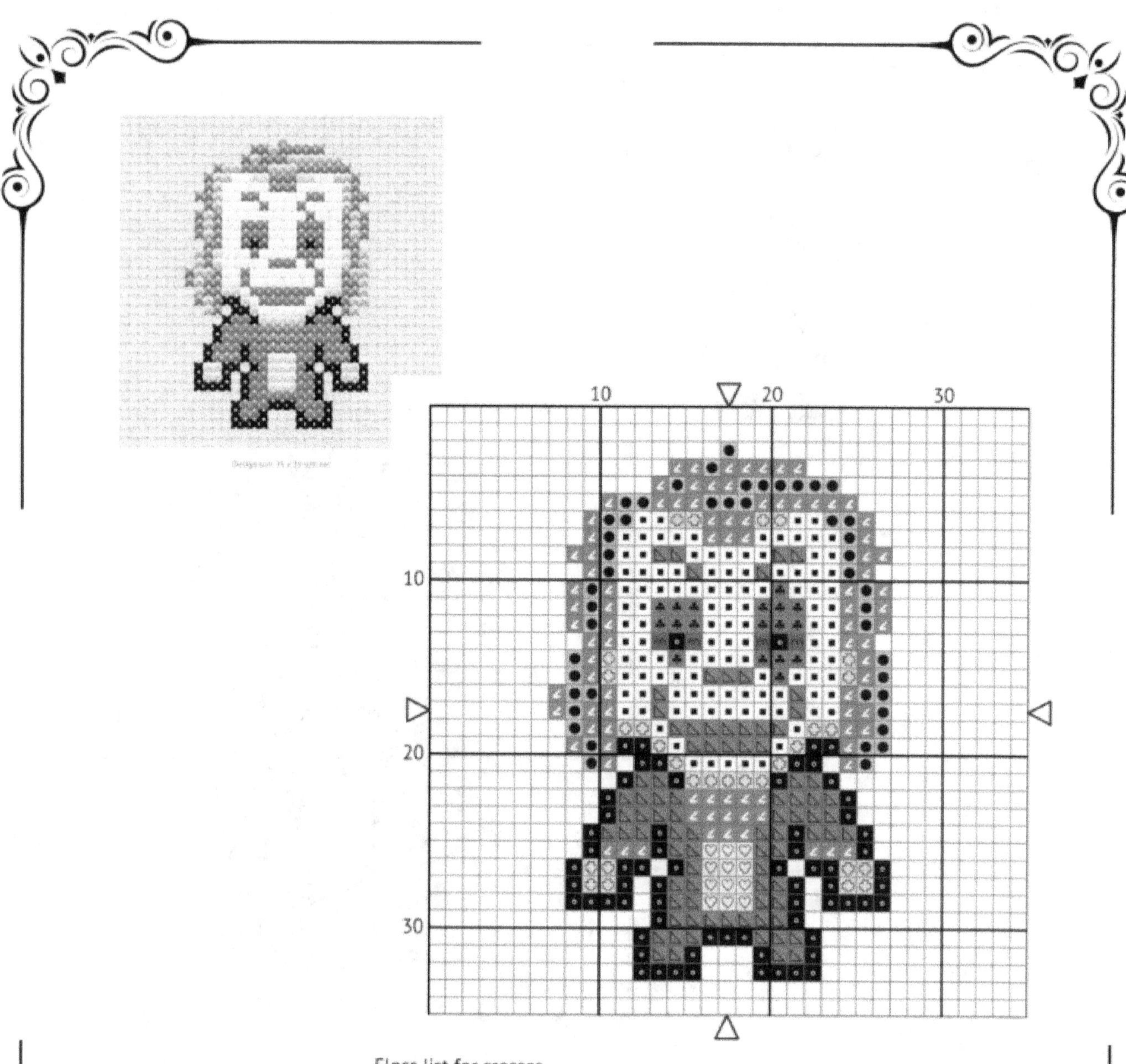

Floss list for crosses

Use 2 strands of thread for cross stitch

N	Symbol		Number	Name	Stitches
1	■	■	DMC B5200	Snow White	116
2	m	m	DMC 33	Fuchsia	4
3	●	●	DMC 164	Forest Green - Light	47
4	♡	♡	DMC 307	Lemon	12
5	◦	◦	DMC 310	Black	69
6	♣	♣	DMC 334	Baby Blue - Medium	18
7	◢	◢	DMC 702	Kelly Green	93
8	✿	✿	DMC 950	Desert Sand - Light	29
9	◁	◁	DMC 3832	Raspberry - Medium	86

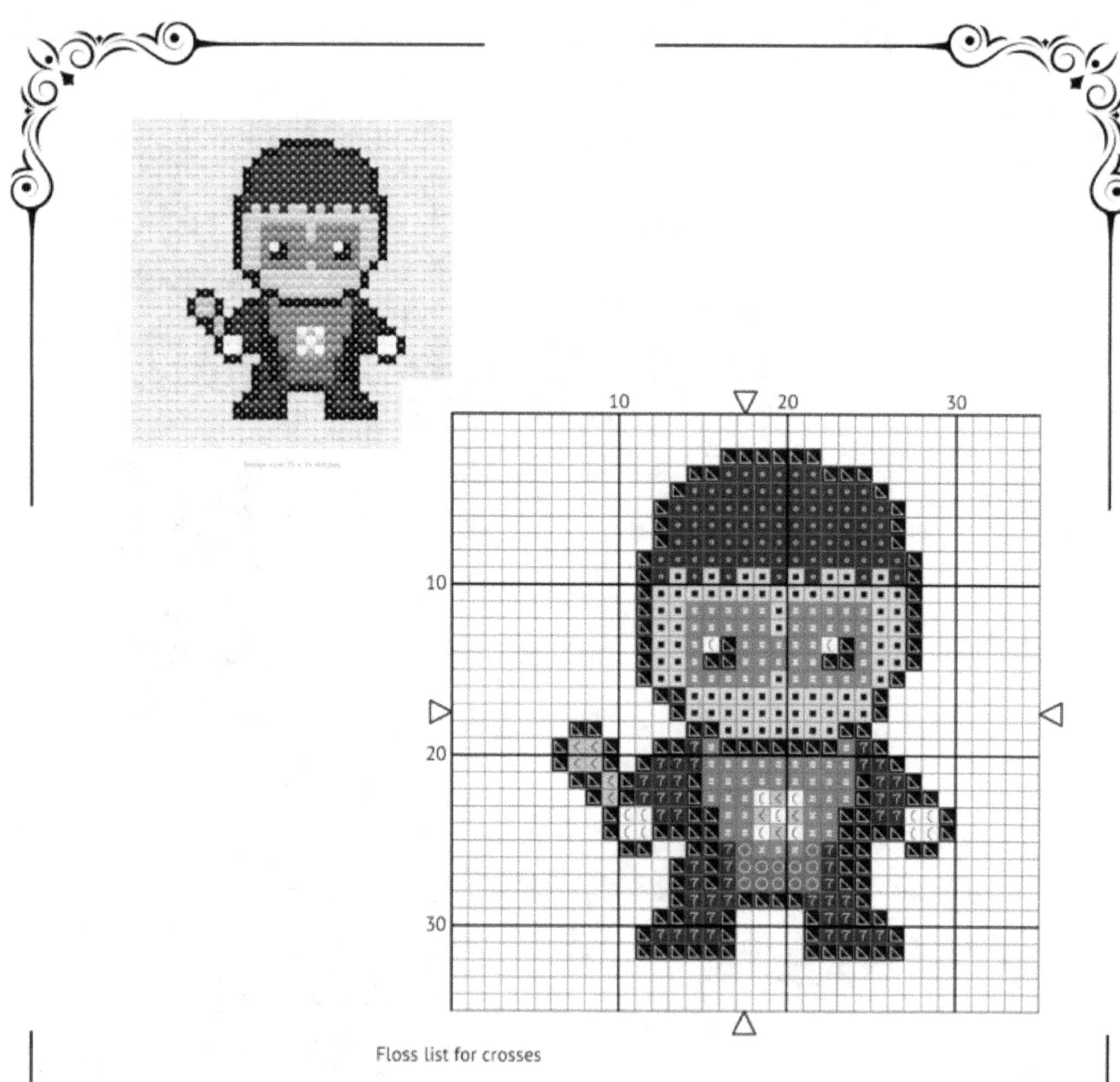

Floss list for crosses

Use 2 strands of thread for cross stitch

N	Symbol		Number	Name	Stitches
1	(	(	DMC B5200	Snow White	15
2	◸	◸	DMC 310	Black	140
3	○	○	DMC 317	Pewter Gray	12
4	7	7	DMC 890	Pistachio Green - Ultra Dark	47
5	◦	◦	DMC 898	Coffee Brown - Very Dark	78
6	<	<	DMC 913	Nile Green - Medium	10
7	≡	≡	DMC 943	Aquamarine - Medium	81
8	■	■	DMC 967	Apricot - Very Light	74

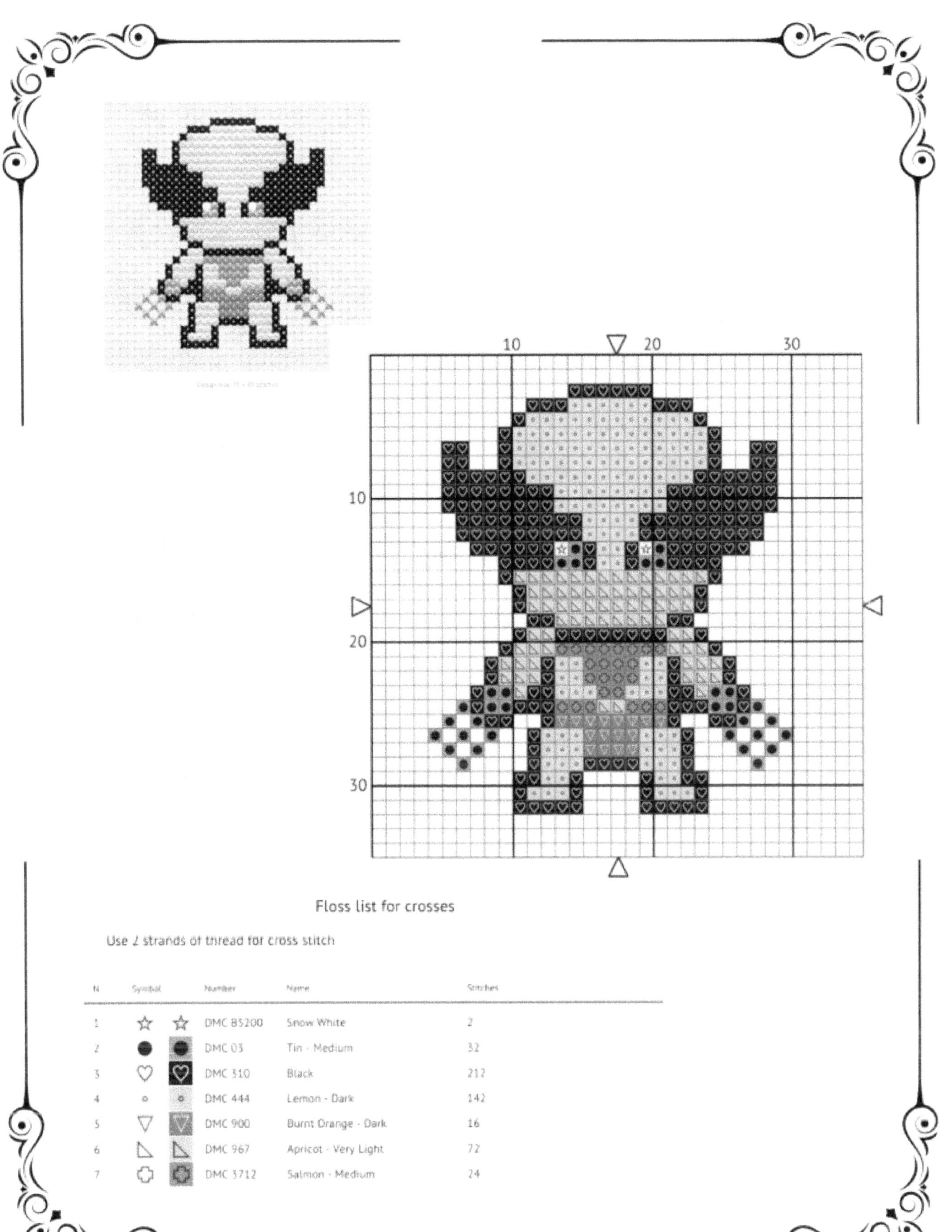

Floss list for crosses

Use 2 strands of thread for cross stitch

N	Symbol		Number	Name	Stitches
1	☆	☆	DMC B5200	Snow White	2
2	●	●	DMC 03	Tin - Medium	32
3	♡	♥	DMC 310	Black	212
4	∘	∘	DMC 444	Lemon - Dark	142
5	▽	▼	DMC 900	Burnt Orange - Dark	16
6	◁	◁	DMC 967	Apricot - Very Light	72
7	⬡	⬡	DMC 3712	Salmon - Medium	24

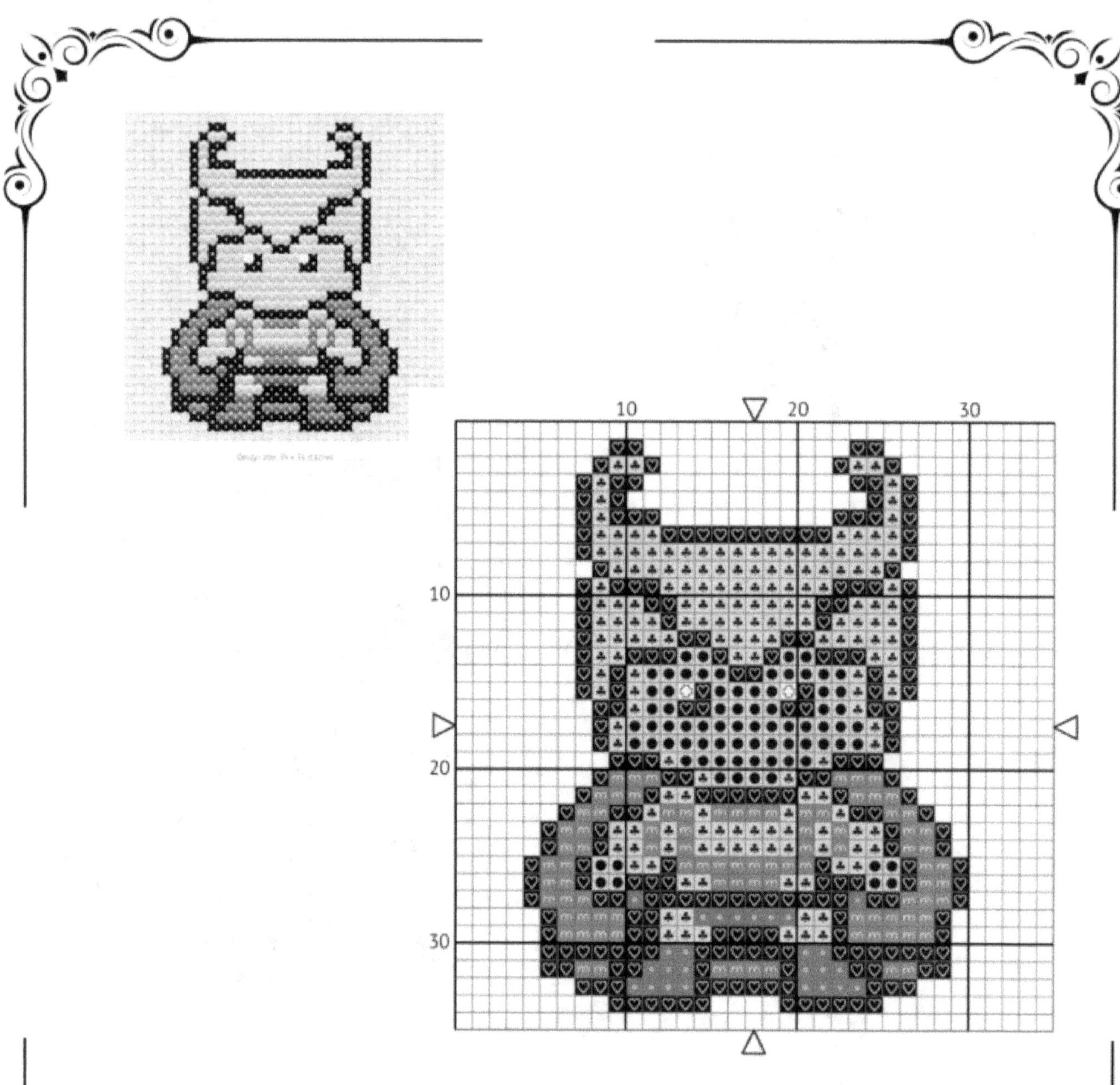

Floss list for crosses

Use 2 strands of thread for cross stitch

N	Symbol		Number	Name	Stitches
1	✛	✛	DMC B5200	Snow White	2
2	♡	♥	DMC 310	Black	238
3	♣	♣	DMC 444	Lemon - Dark	182
4	m	m	DMC 943	Aquamarine - Medium	92
5	●	●	DMC 967	Apricot - Very Light	78
6	○	○	DMC 3347	Yellow Green - Medium	26

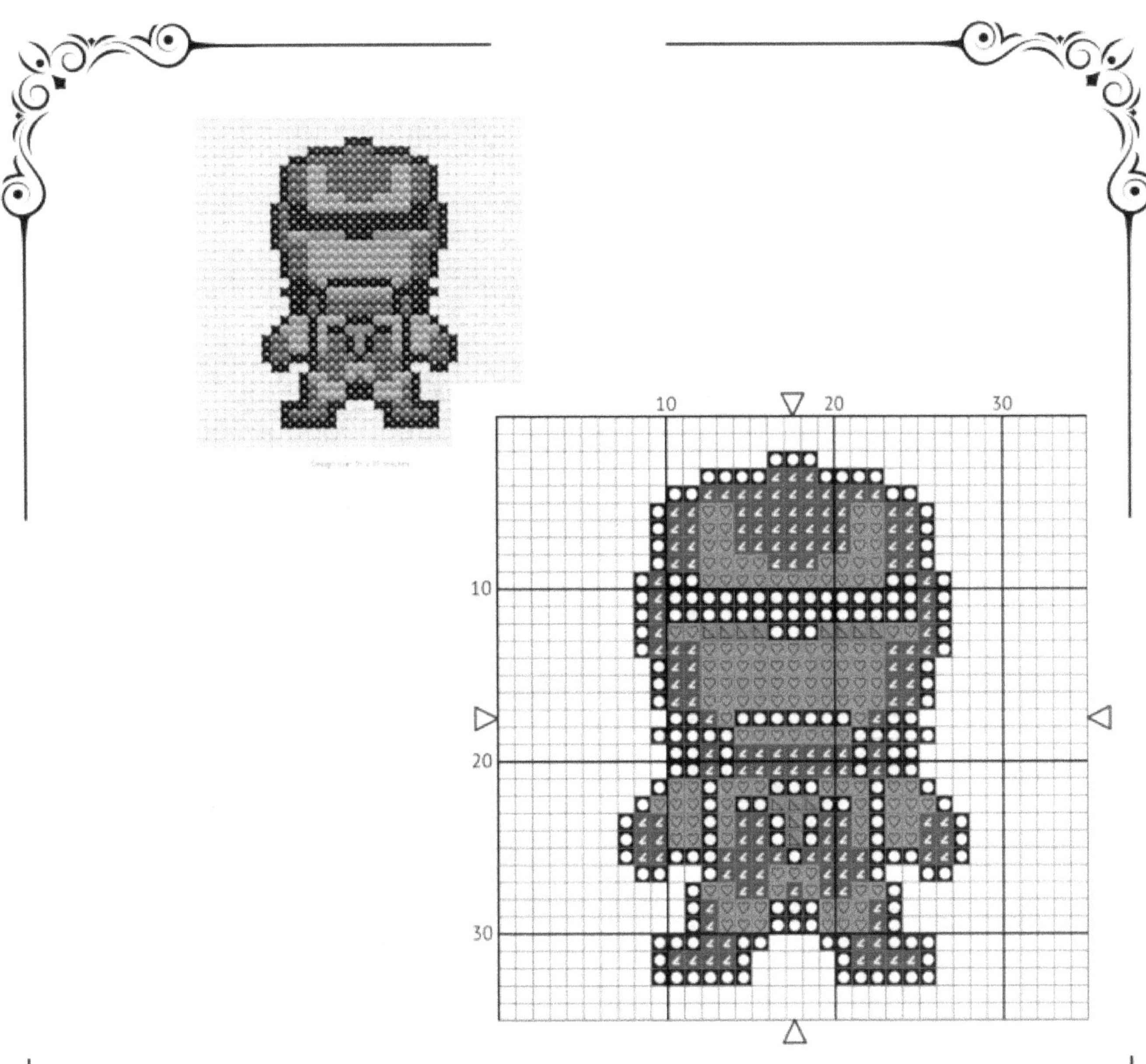

Floss list for crosses

Use 2 strands of thread for cross stitch

N	Symbol	Number	Name	Stitches
1	● ◻	DMC 310	Black	189
2	◢ ◢	DMC 413	Pewter Gray - Dark	155
3	♡ ♡	DMC 952	Antique Blue - Light	139
4	◺ ◺	DMC 3832	Raspberry - Medium	13

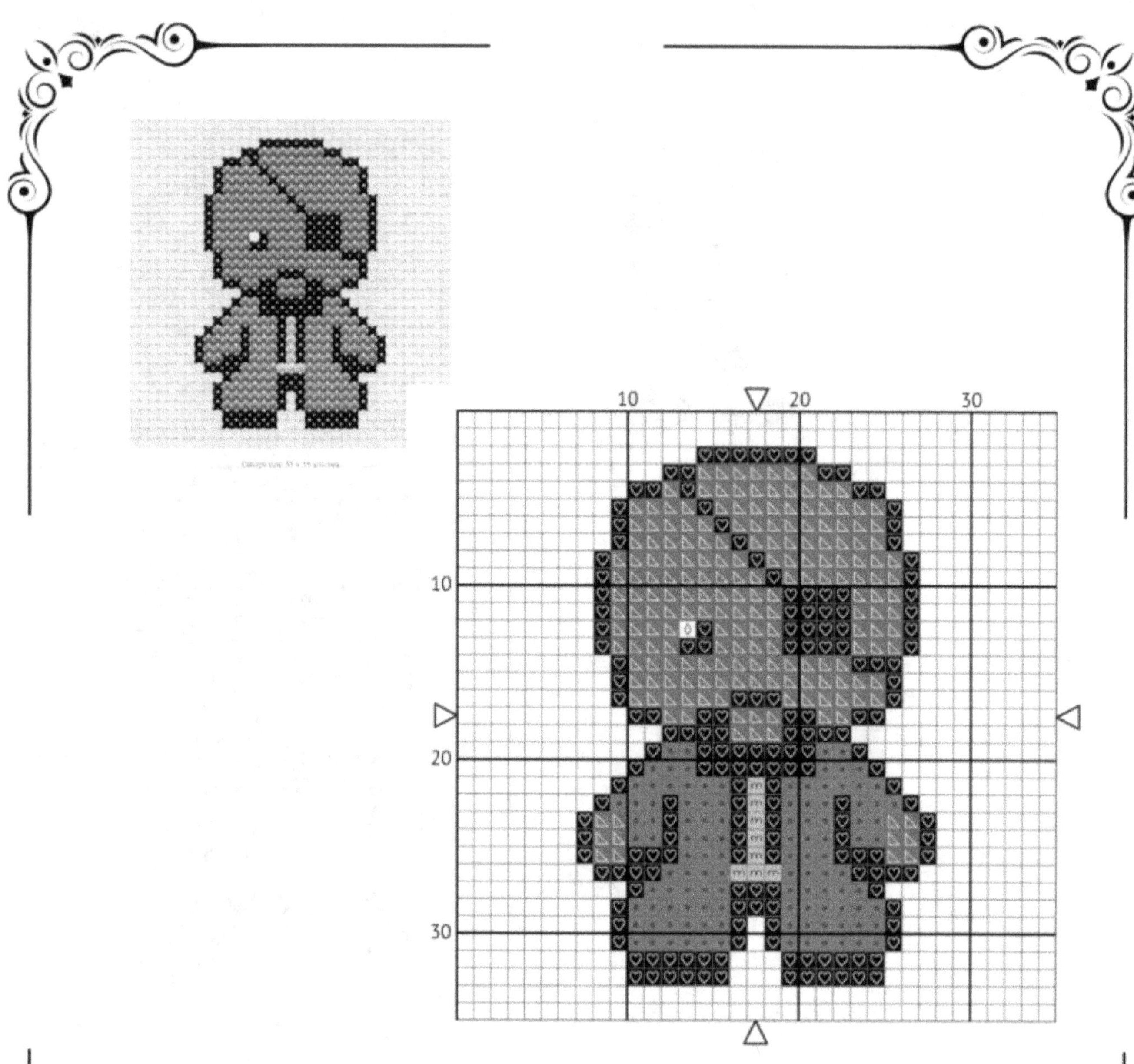

Floss list for crosses

Use 2 strands of thread for cross stitch

N	Symbol		Number	Name	Stitches
1	◊	◊	DMC B5200	Snow White	1
2	♡	♥	DMC 310	Black	185
3	o	a	DMC 926	Gray Green - Medium	114
4	m	m	DMC 928	Gray Green - Very Light	8
5	◺	◣	DMC 3829	Old Gold - Very Dark	201

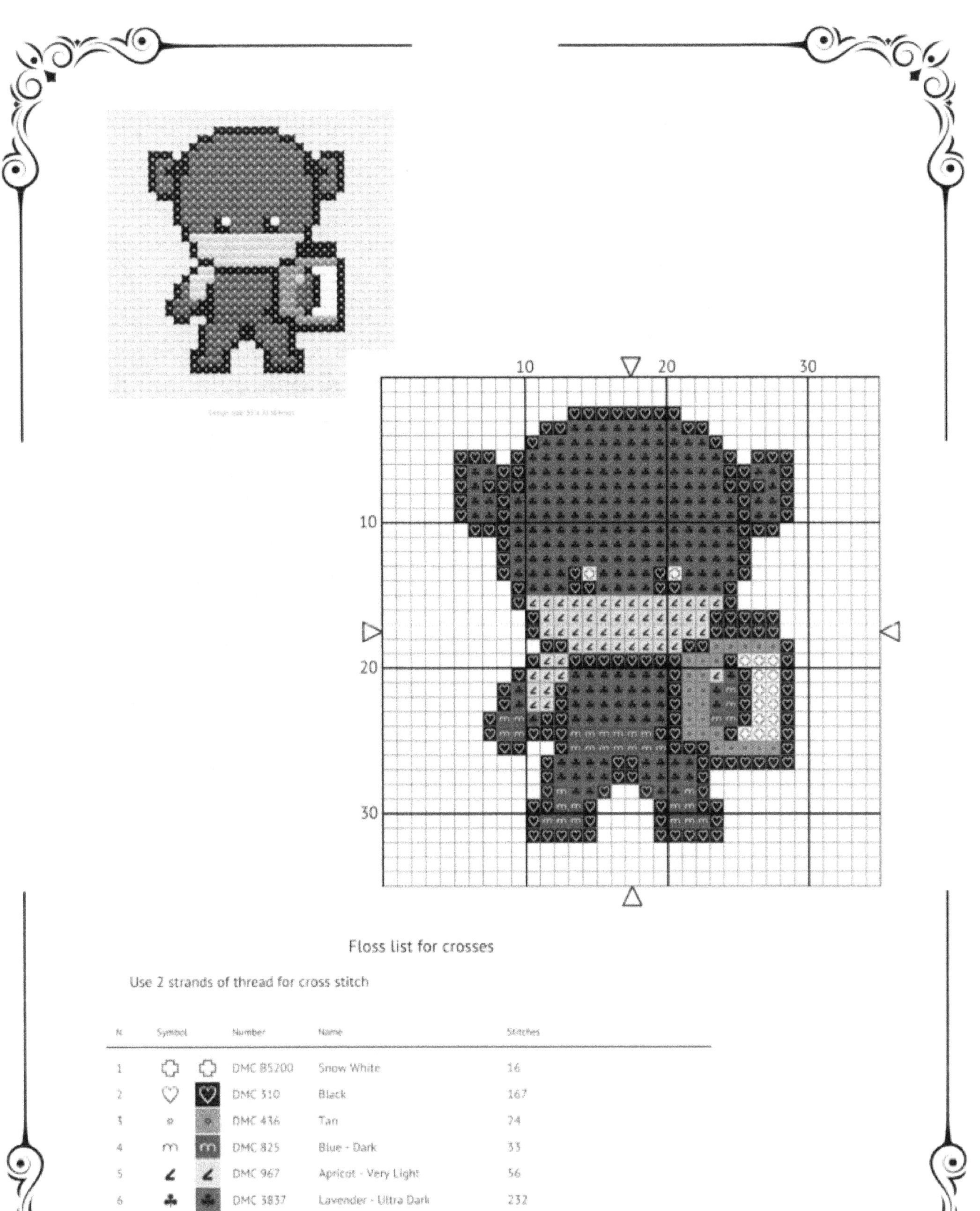

Floss list for crosses

Use 2 strands of thread for cross stitch

N	Symbol		Number	Name	Stitches
1	✤	✤	DMC B5200	Snow White	16
2	♡	♥	DMC 310	Black	167
3	◦	◦	DMC 436	Tan	24
4	m	m	DMC 825	Blue - Dark	33
5	◢	◢	DMC 967	Apricot - Very Light	56
6	♣	♣	DMC 3837	Lavender - Ultra Dark	232

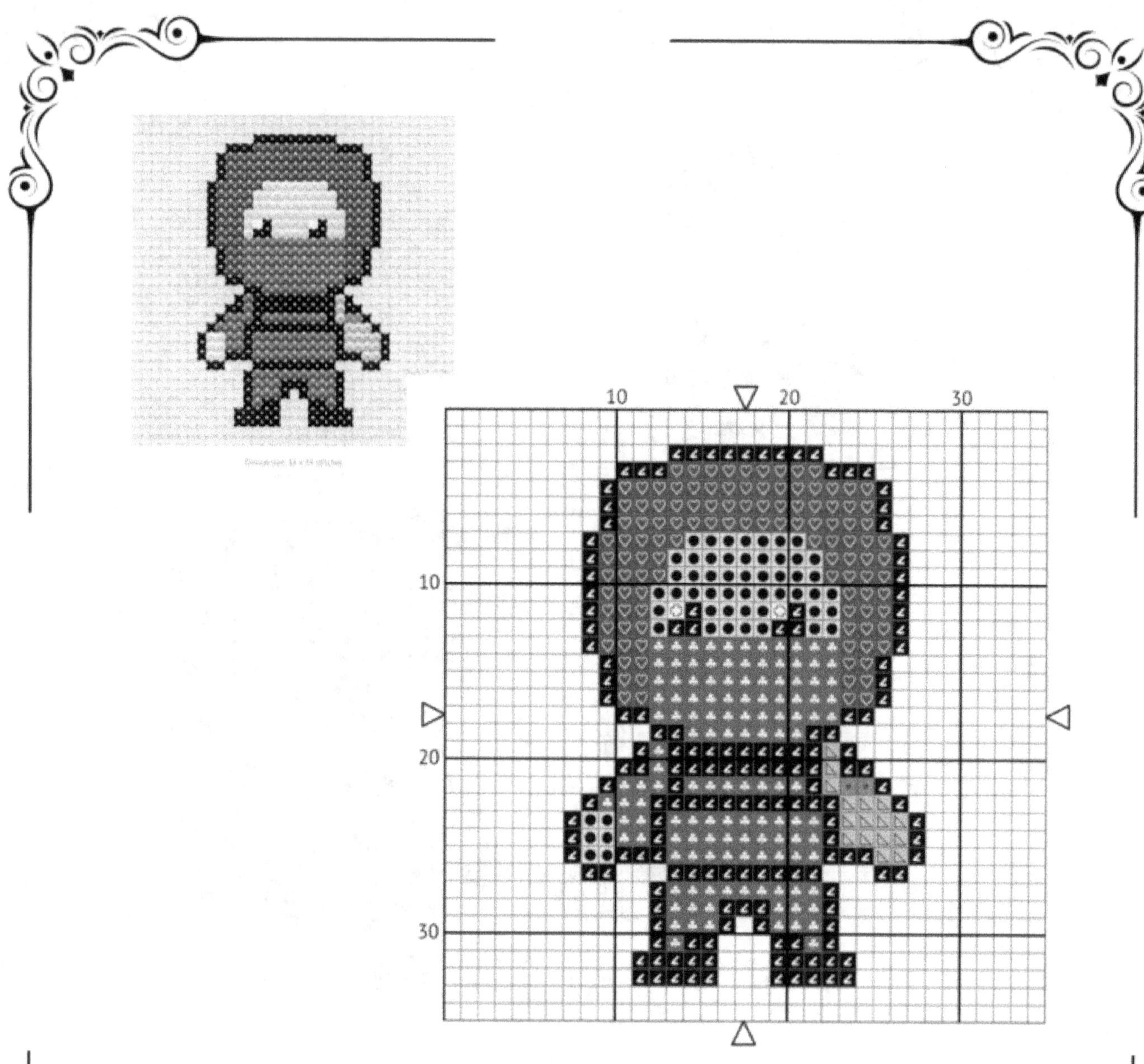

Floss list for crosses

Use 2 strands of thread for cross stitch

N	Symbol		Number	Name	Stitches
1			DMC B5200	Snow White	2
2			DMC 310	Black	162
3			DMC 350	Coral - Medium	2
4			DMC 779	Cocoa - Dark	116
5			DMC 928	Gray Green - Very Light	16
6			DMC 3768	Gray Green - Dark	131
7			DMC 3774	Desert Sand - Very Light	56

IRON MAN

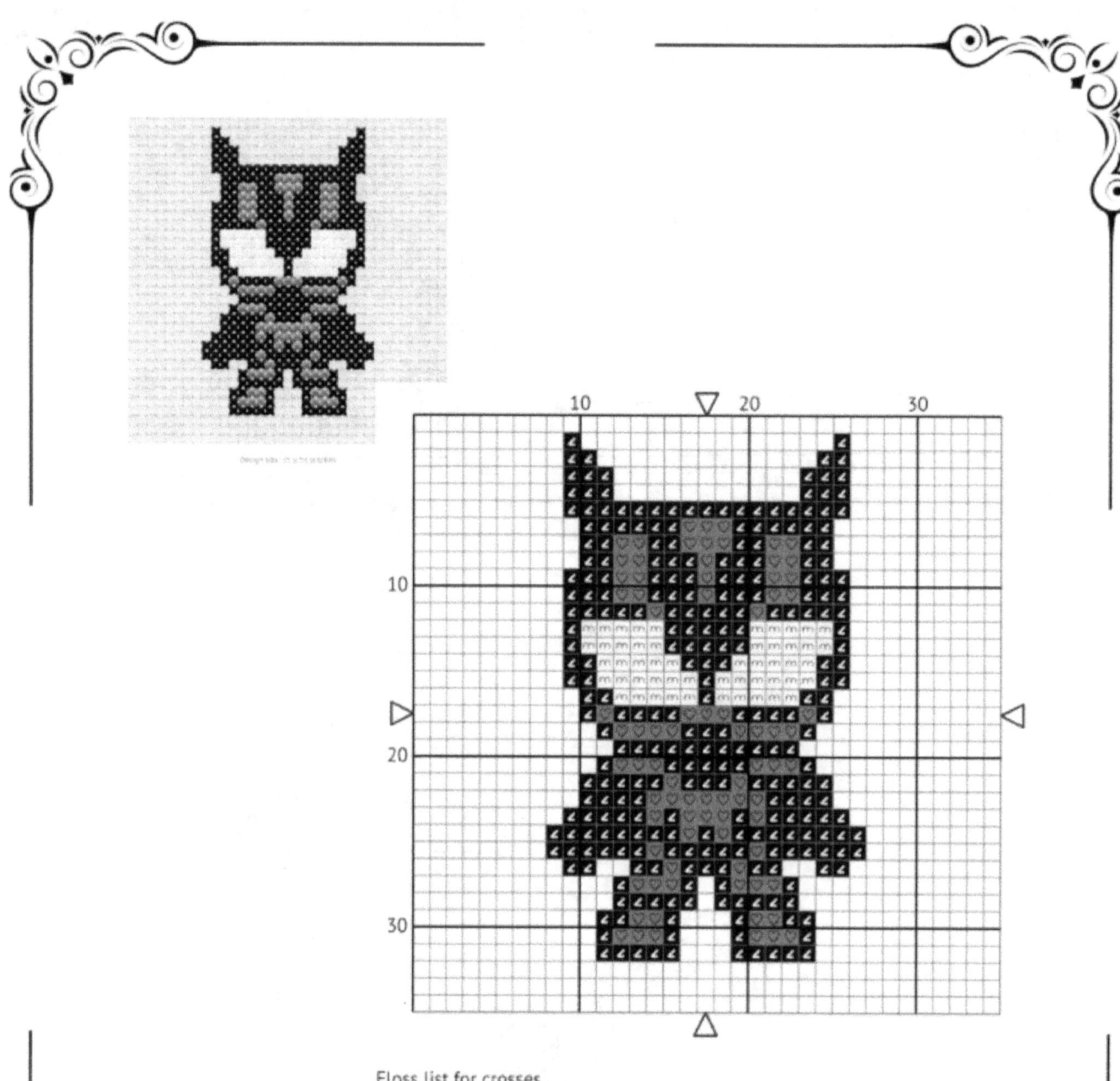

Floss list for crosses

Use 2 strands of thread for cross stitch

N	Symbol		Number	Name	Stitches
1	m	m	DMC B5200	Snow White	52
2	∠	∠	DMC 310	Black	280
3	♡	♡	DMC 926	Gray Green - Medium	82

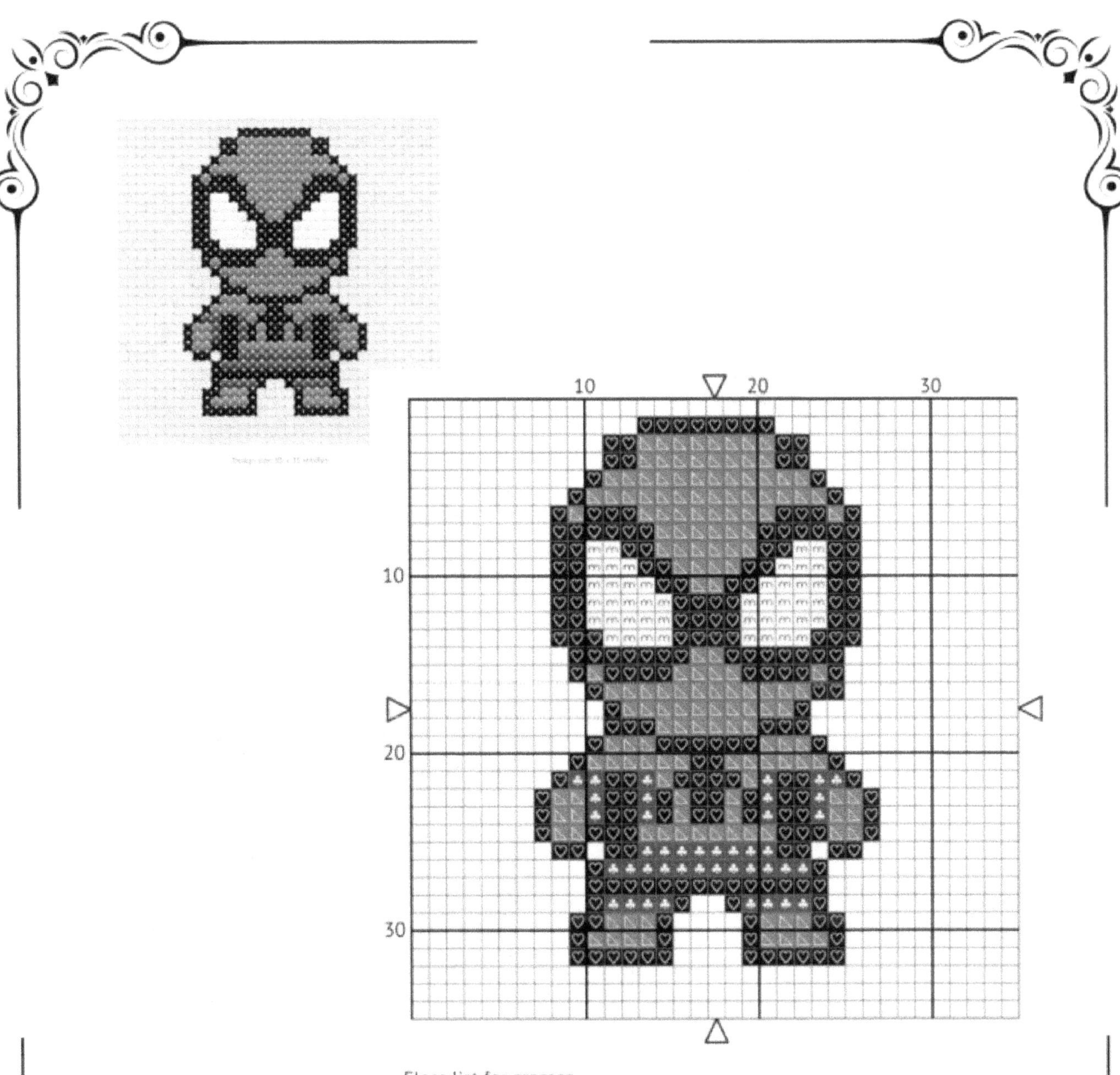

Floss list for crosses

Use 2 strands of thread for cross stitch

N	Symbol		Number	Name	Stitches
1	m	m	DMC B5200	Snow White	46
2	♡		DMC 310	Black	225
3	♣		DMC 825	Blue - Dark	42
4	◺		DMC 900	Burnt Orange - Dark	164

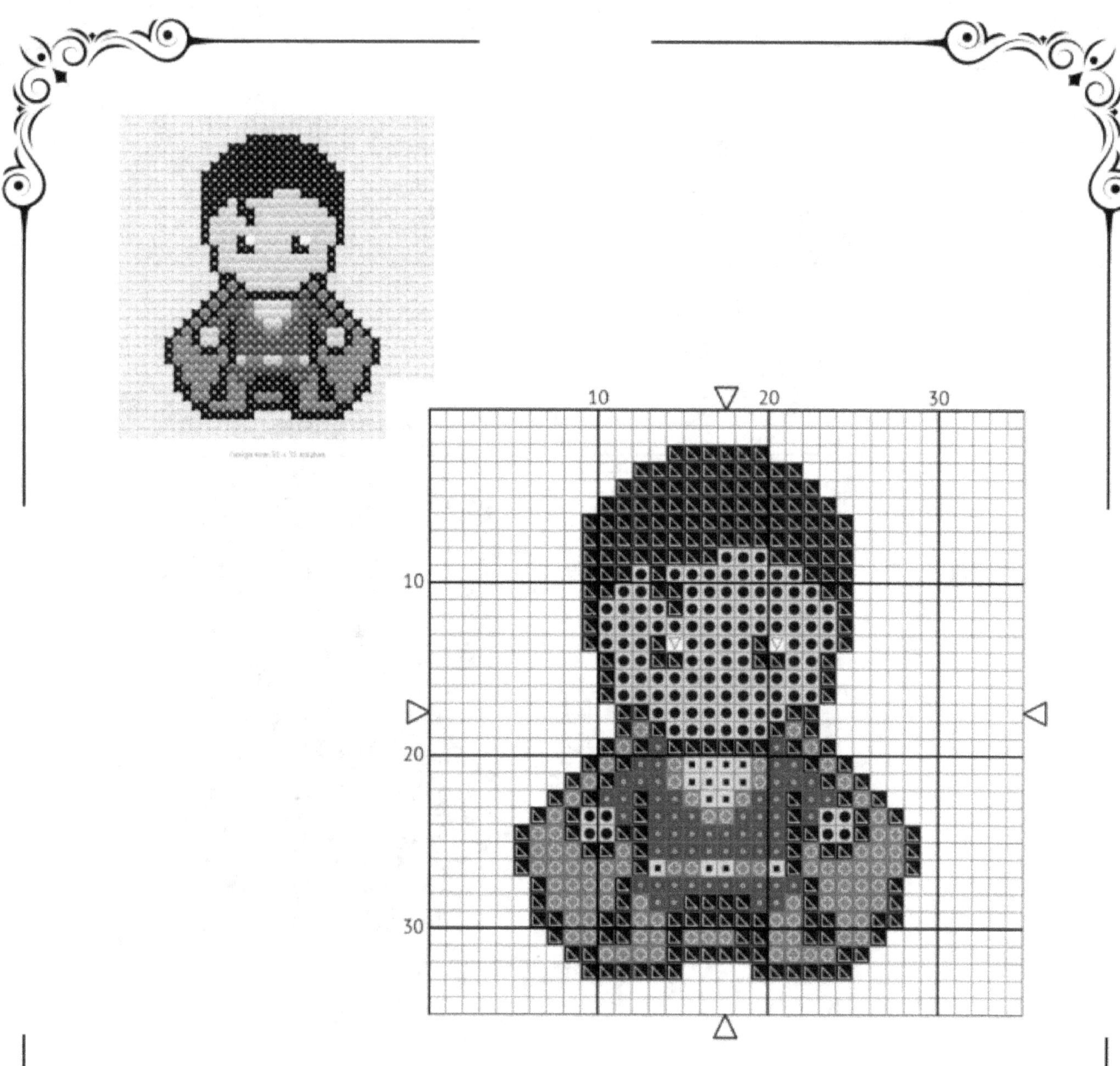

Floss list for crosses

Use 2 strands of thread for cross stitch

N	Symbol		Number	Name	Stitches
1	▽	▽	DMC B5200	Snow White	2
2	◺	◣	DMC 310	Black	234
3	■	■	DMC 444	Lemon - Dark	14
4	○	◉	DMC 825	Blue - Dark	58
5	✛	✛	DMC 900	Burnt Orange - Dark	93
6	●	●	DMC 967	Apricot - Very Light	113

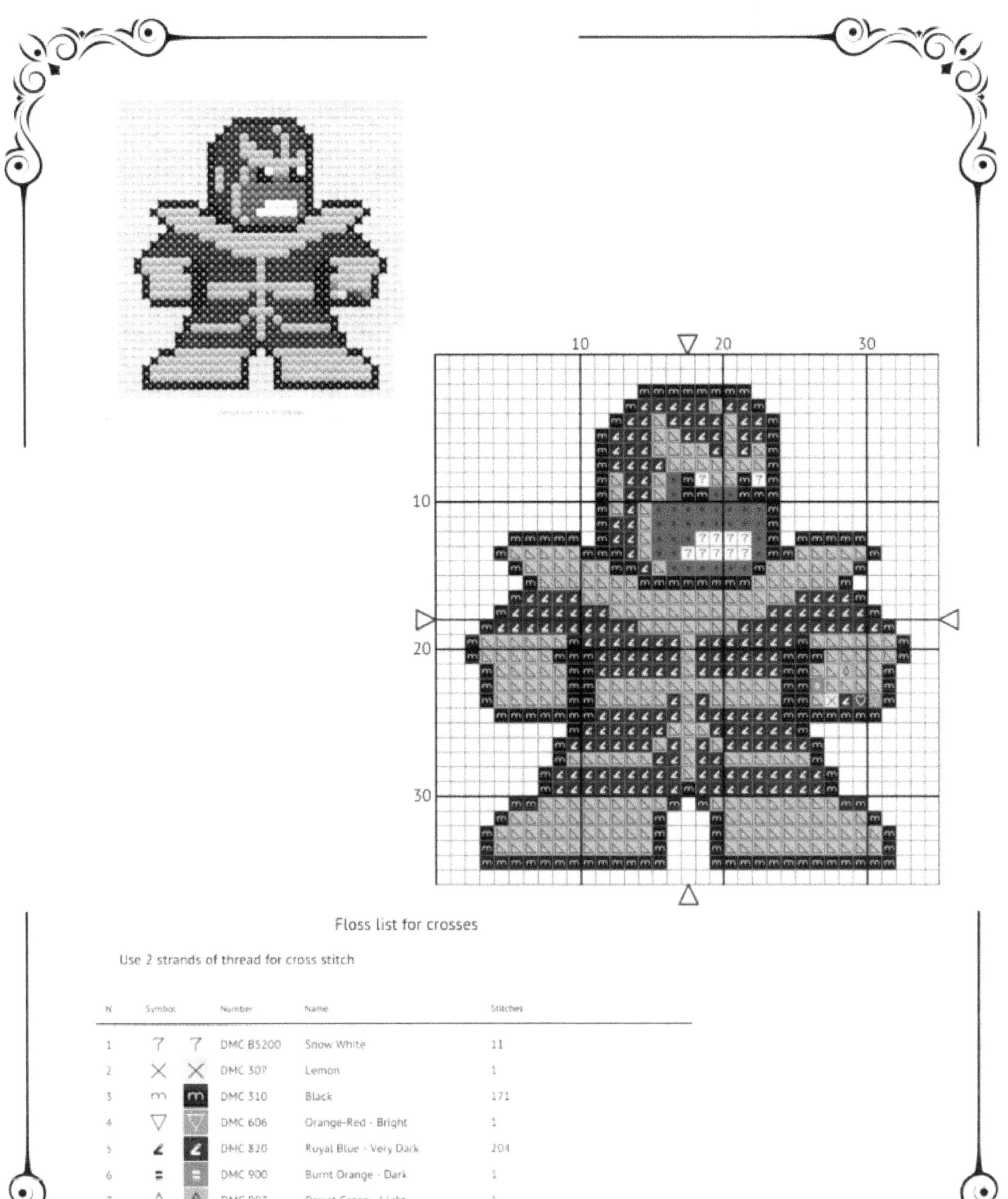

Floss list for crosses

Use 2 strands of thread for cross stitch

N	Symbol		Number	Name	Stitches
1	7	7	DMC B5200	Snow White	11
2	×	×	DMC 307	Lemon	1
3	m	m	DMC 310	Black	171
4	▽	▽	DMC 606	Orange-Red - Bright	1
5	◢	◢	DMC 820	Royal Blue - Very Dark	204
6	=	=	DMC 900	Burnt Orange - Dark	1
7	◊	◊	DMC 907	Parrot Green - Light	1
8	◺	◺	DMC 972	Canary - Deep	275
9	♡	♡	DMC 3834	Grape - Dark	1
10	○	○	DMC 3837	Lavender - Ultra Dark	33

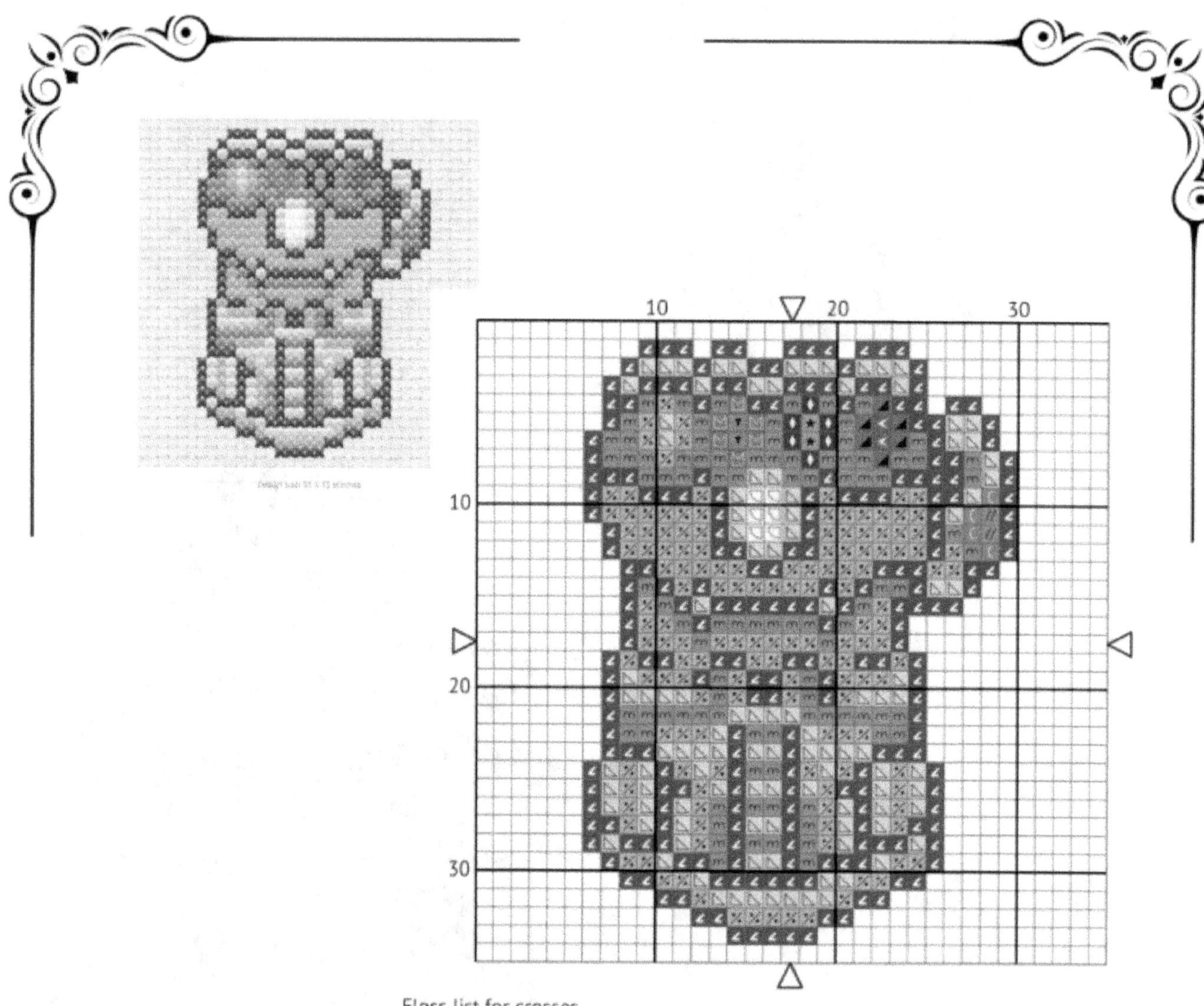

Floss list for crosses

Use 2 strands of thread for cross stitch

N	Symbol		Number	Name	Stitches
1			DMC B5200	Snow White	6
2			DMC 208	Lavender - Very Dark	6
3			DMC 444	Lemon - Dark	110
4			DMC 702	Kelly Green	4
5			DMC 741	Tangerine - Medium	146
6			DMC 792	Cornflower Blue - Dark	6
7			DMC 816	Garnet	229
8			DMC 817	Coral Red - Very Dark	6
9			DMC 917	Plum - Medium	2
10			DMC 3328	Salmon - Dark	2
11			DMC 3845	Bright Turquoise - Medium	2
12			DMC 3851	Bright Green - Light	2
13			DMC 3853	Autumn Gold - Dark	95

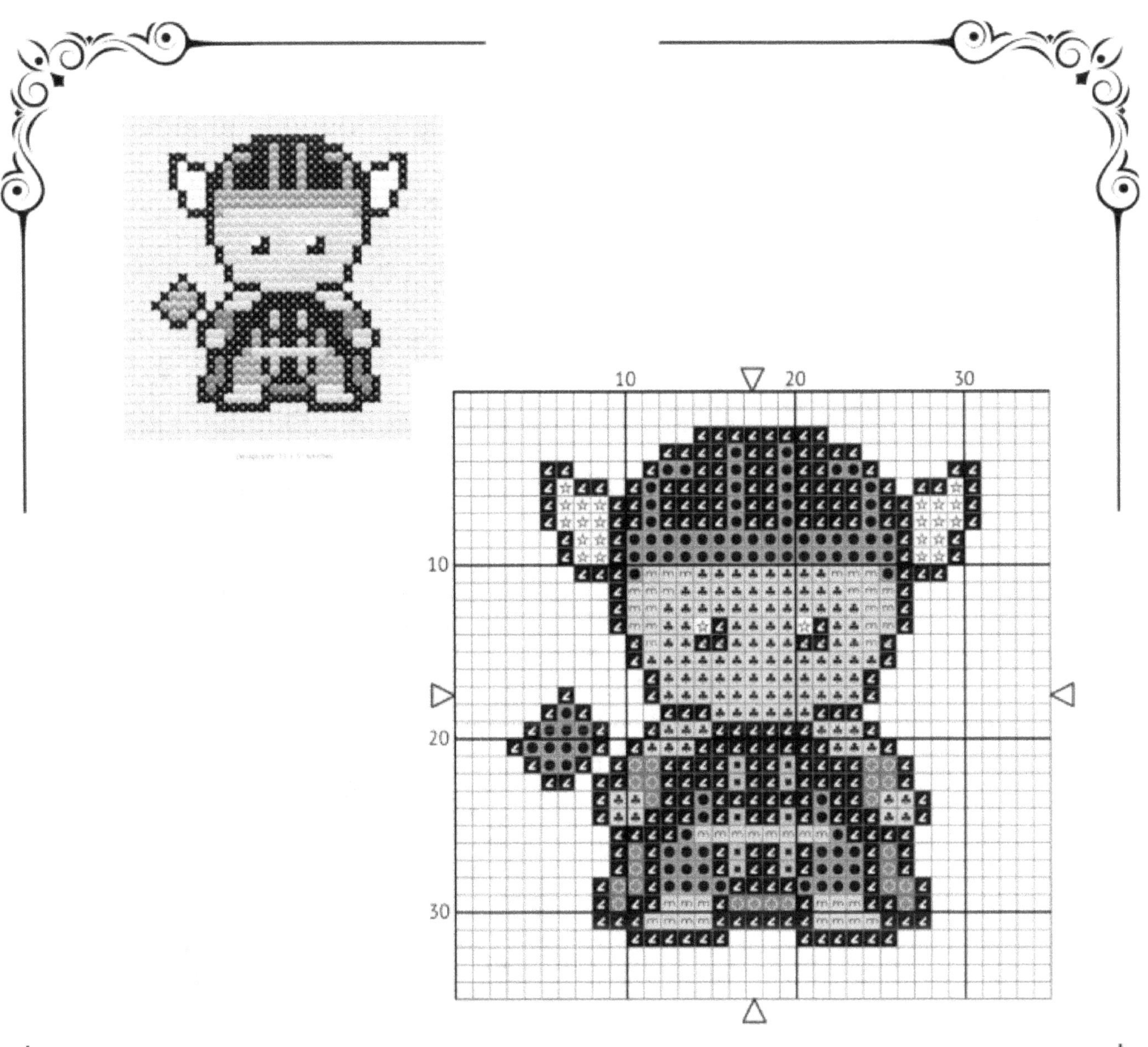

Floss list for crosses

Use 2 strands of thread for cross stitch

N	Symbol		Number	Name	Stitches
1	☆	☆	DMC B5200	Snow White	24
2	●	●	DMC 03	Tin - Medium	90
3	⟋	⟋	DMC 310	Black	262
4	m	m	DMC 444	Lemon - Dark	44
5	✿	✿	DMC 900	Burnt Orange - Dark	24
6	♣	♣	DMC 967	Apricot - Very Light	110
7	■	■	DMC 3766	Peacock Blue - Light	10

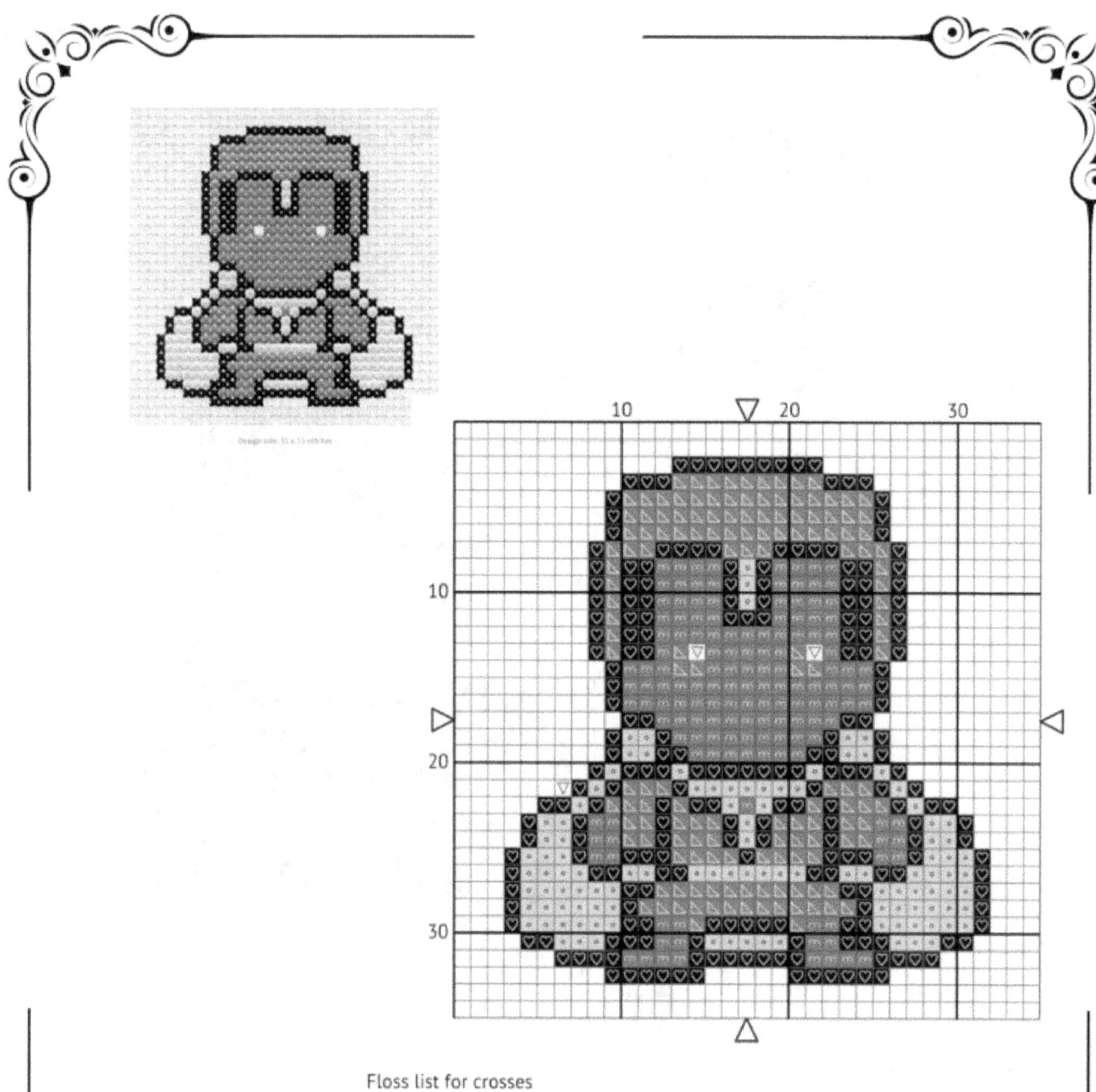

Floss list for crosses

Use 2 strands of thread for cross stitch

N	Symbol		Number	Name	Stitches
1	▽	▽	DMC B5200	Snow White	3
2	♡	♥	DMC 310	Black	226
3	o	o	DMC 444	Lemon - Dark	110
4	m	m	DMC 900	Burnt Orange - Dark	147
5	◺	◺	DMC 943	Aquamarine - Medium	149

Floss list for crosses

Use 2 strands of thread for cross stitch

N	Symbol		Number	Name	Stitches
1	■	■	DMC B5200	Snow White	27
2	♡	♥	DMC 310	Black	229
3	♣	♣	DMC 444	Lemon - Dark	67
4	◹	◹	DMC 825	Blue - Dark	14
5	✿	✿	DMC 829	Golden Olive - Very Dark	17
6	m	m	DMC 900	Burnt Orange - Dark	32
7	●	●	DMC 967	Apricot - Very Light	121
8	◦	p	DMC 3766	Peacock Blue - Light	9

Floss list for crosses

Use 2 strands of thread for cross stitch

N	Symbol		Number	Name	Stitches
1	o	o	DMC B5200	Snow White	2
2	m	m	DMC 03	Tin - Medium	14
3	◢	◢	DMC 310	Black	197
4	♣	♣	DMC 890	Pistachio Green - Ultra Dark	76
5	♡	♡	DMC 900	Burnt Orange - Dark	136
6	◺	◺	DMC 3779	Rosewood - Very Light	144

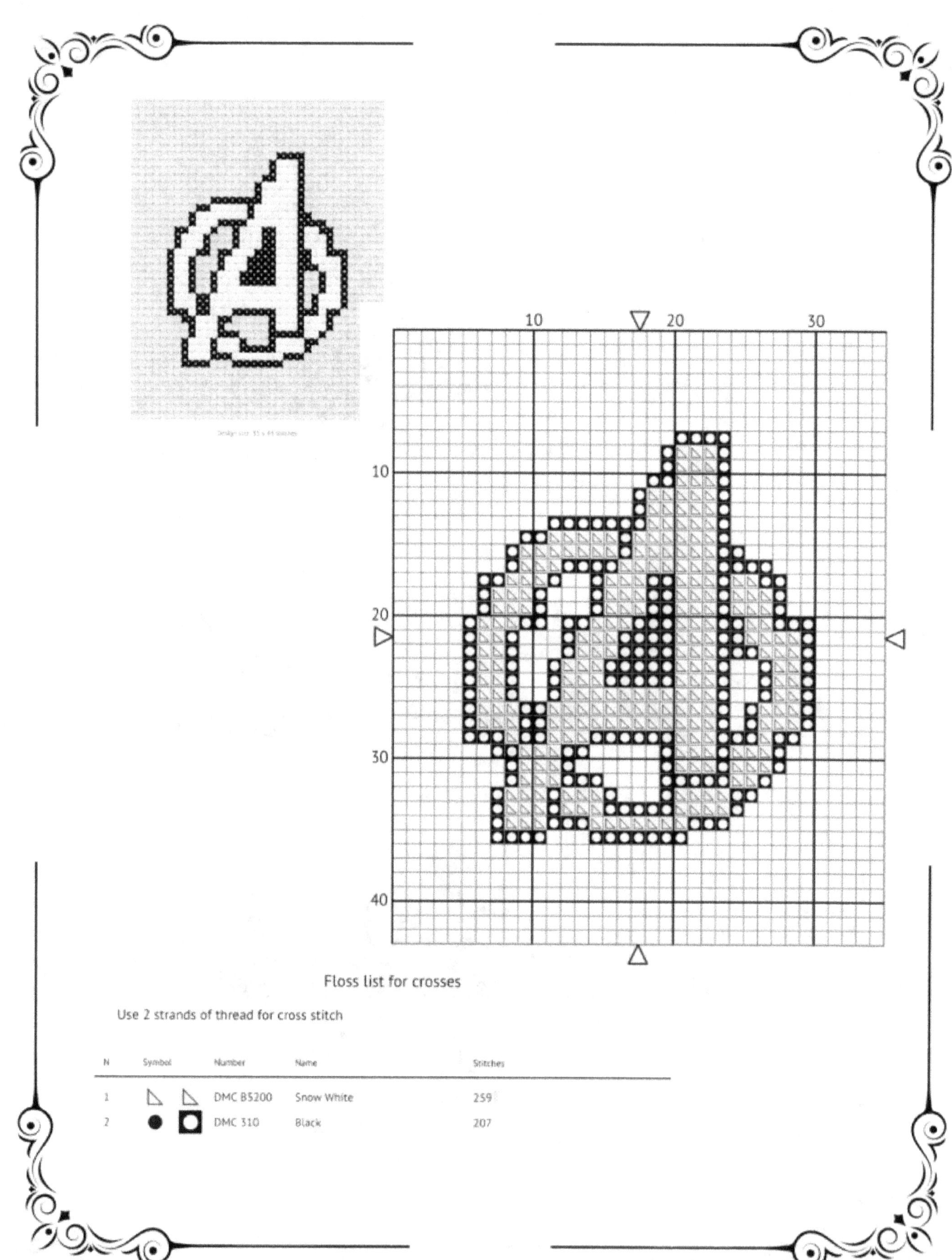

Floss list for crosses

Use 2 strands of thread for cross stitch

N	Symbol		Number	Name	Stitches
1	△	△	DMC B5200	Snow White	259
2	●	◪	DMC 310	Black	207

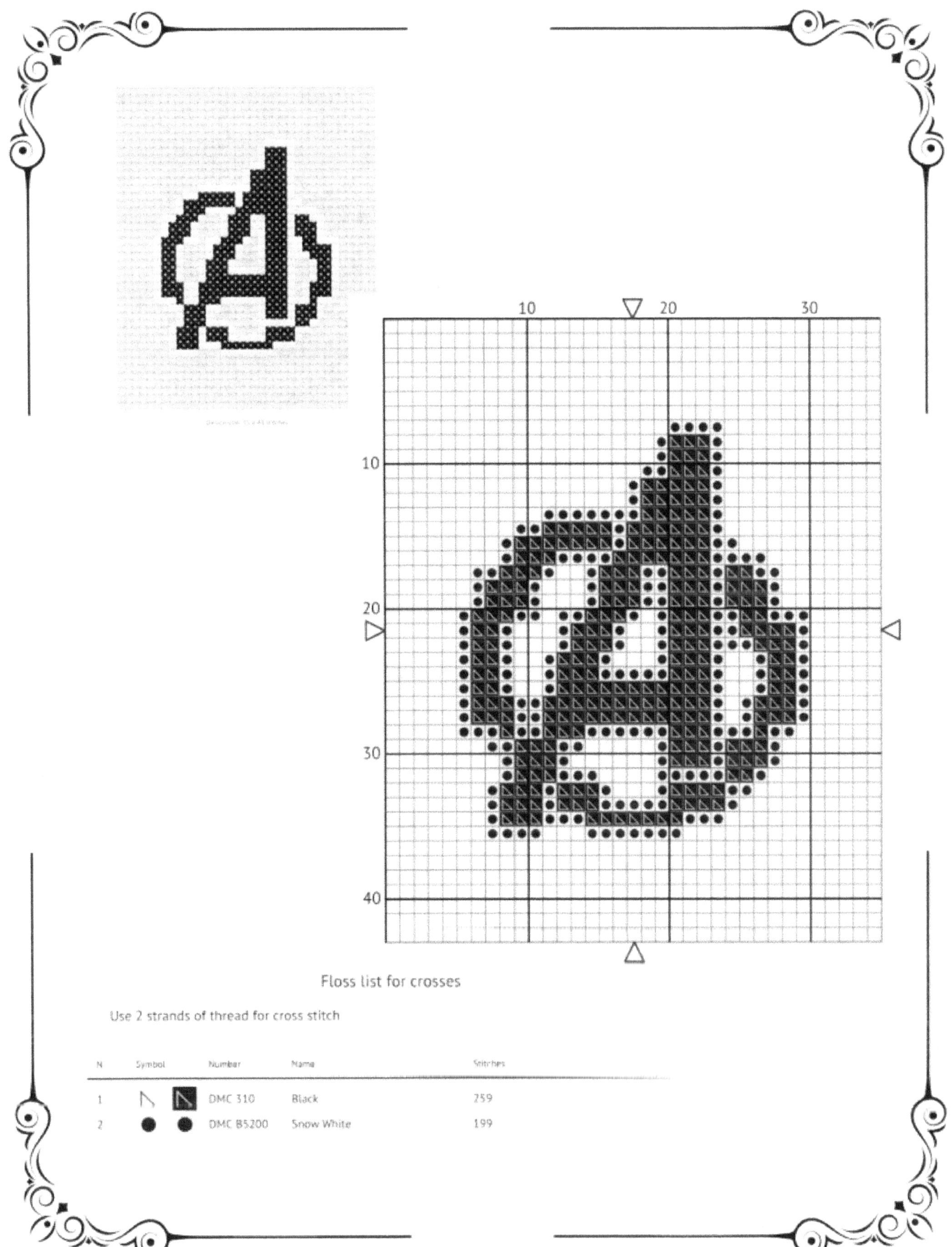

Floss list for crosses

Use 2 strands of thread for cross stitch

N	Symbol		Number	Name	Stitches
1	◹	◩	DMC 310	Black	259
2	●	●	DMC B5200	Snow White	199

Design size: 90 x 118 stitches

Floss list for crosses

Use 2 strands of thread for cross stitch

N	Symbol		Number	Name	Stitches
1	◊	◊	DMC B5200	Snow White	24
2	◺	◺	DMC 03	Tin - Medium	266
3	◢	◢	DMC 310	Black	1442
4	=	=	DMC 543	Beige - Ultra Very Light	636
5	✿	✿	DMC 612	Drab Brown - Light	596
6	♡	♡	DMC 676	Old Gold - Light	210
7	▽	▽	DMC 3013	Khaki Green - Light	374
8	m	m	DMC 3347	Yellow Green - Medium	169

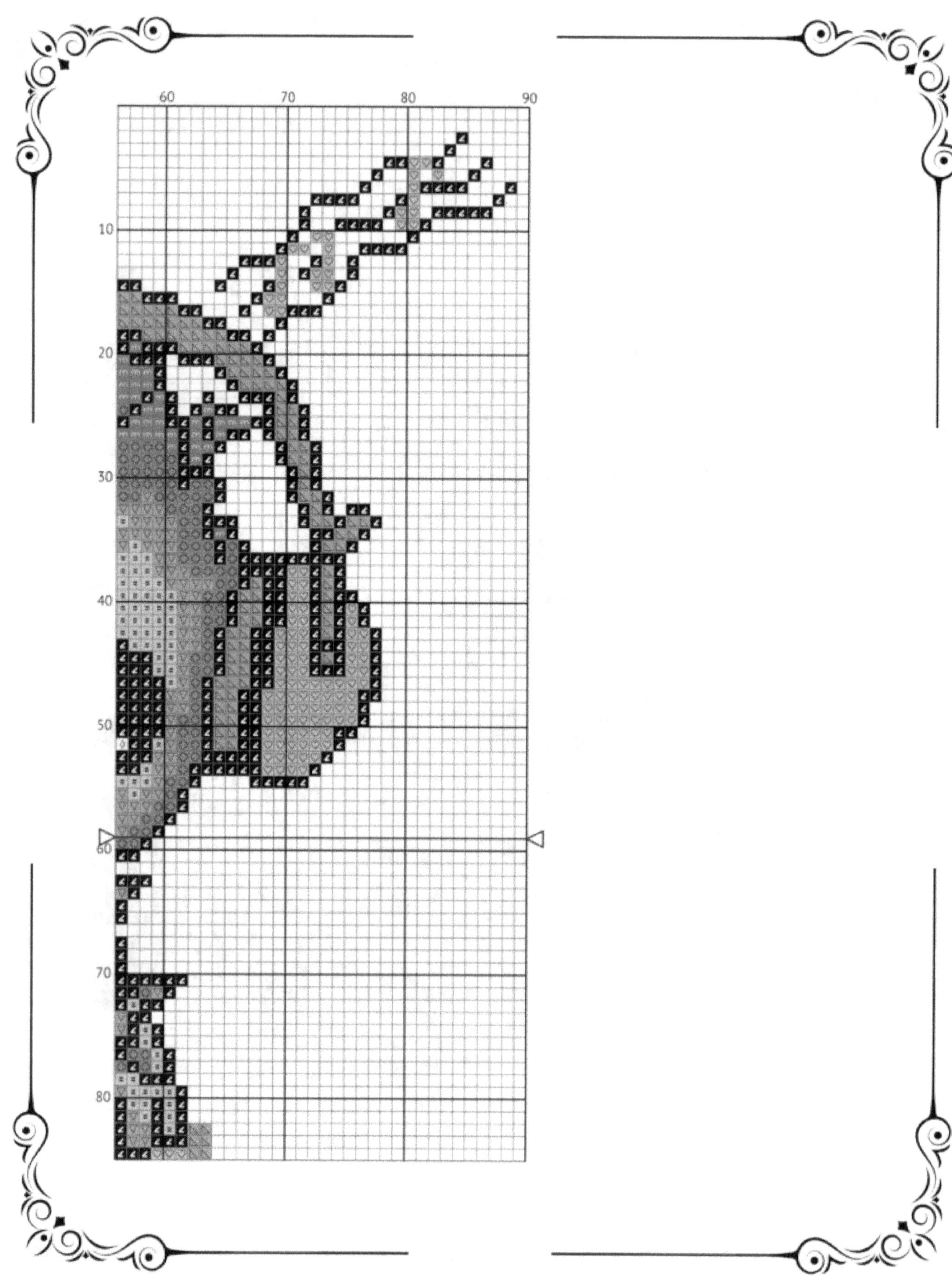

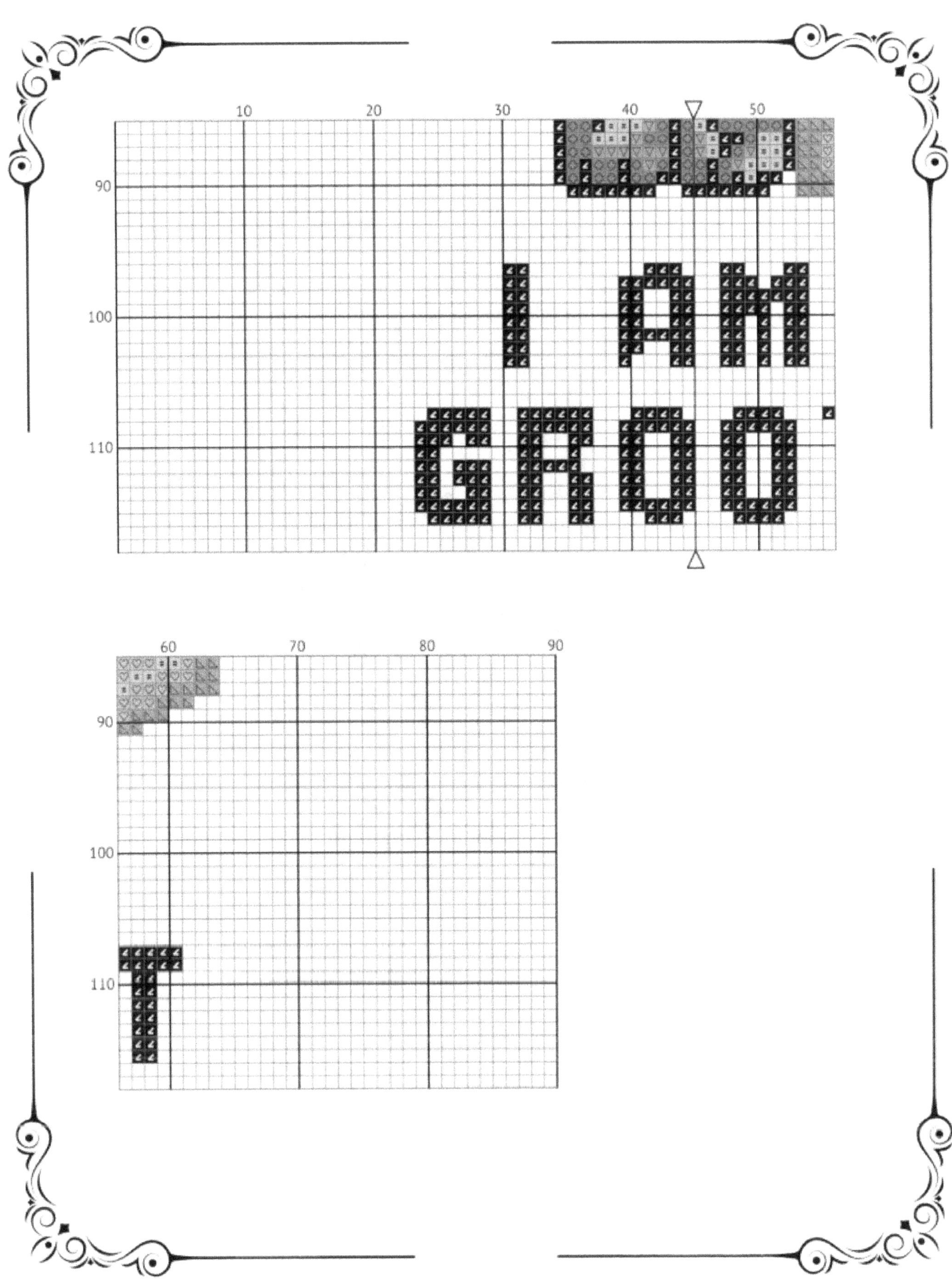

Design size: 70 x 120 stitches

Floss list for crosses

Use 2 strands of thread for cross stitch

N	Symbol		Number	Name	Stitches
1	✂	✂	DMC B5200	Snow White	106
2	◢	◢	DMC 310	Black	2019
3	♡	♡	DMC 471	Avocado Green - Very Light	248
4	◺	◺	DMC 610	Drab Brown - Dark	3513

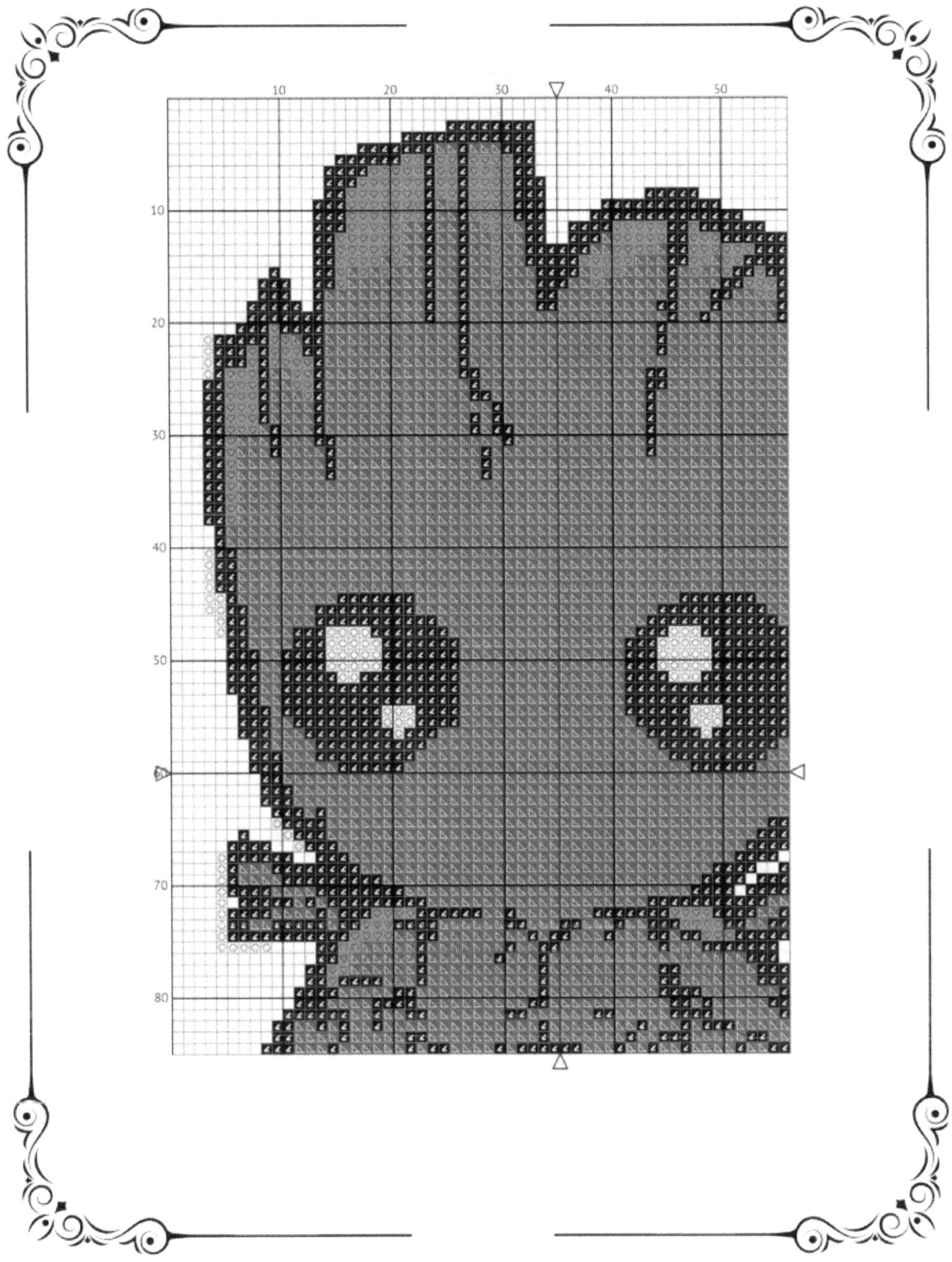

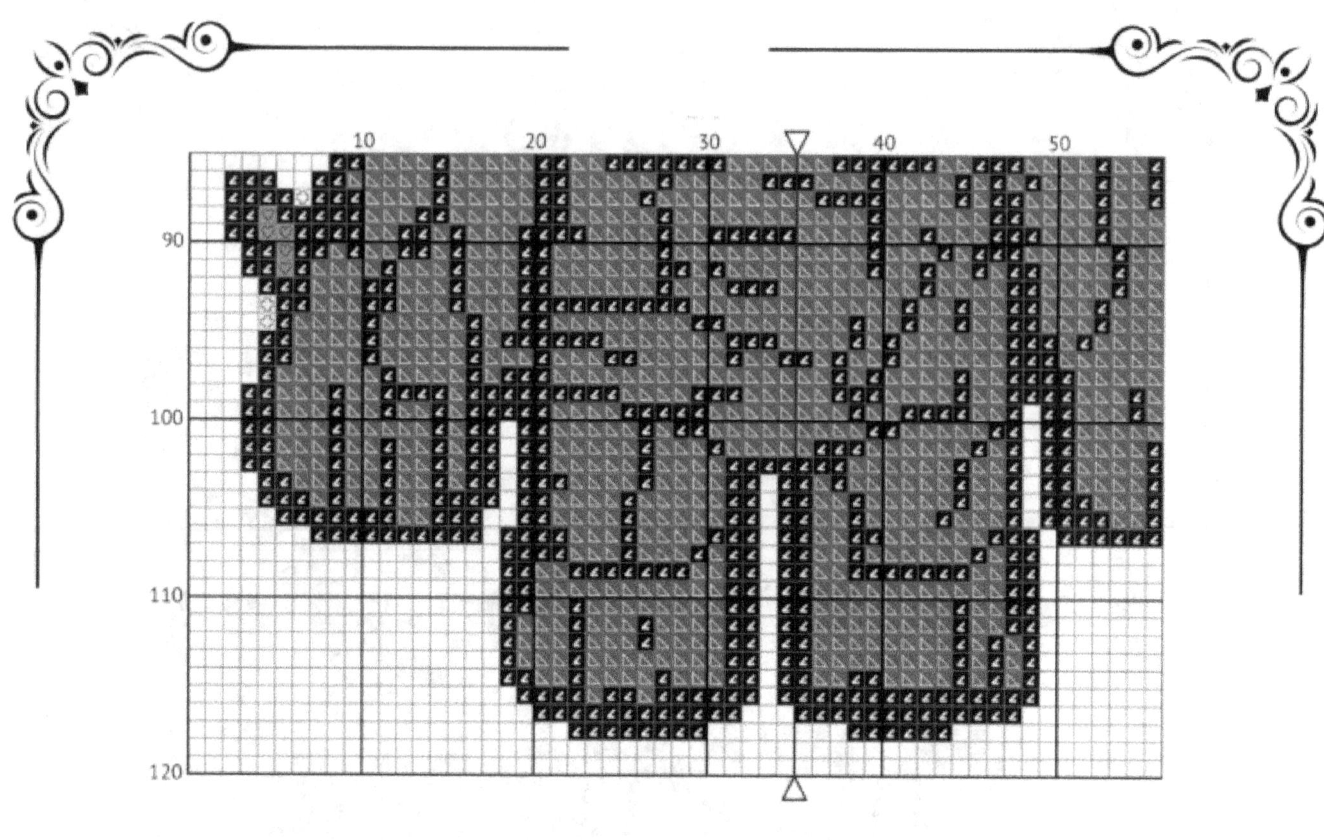

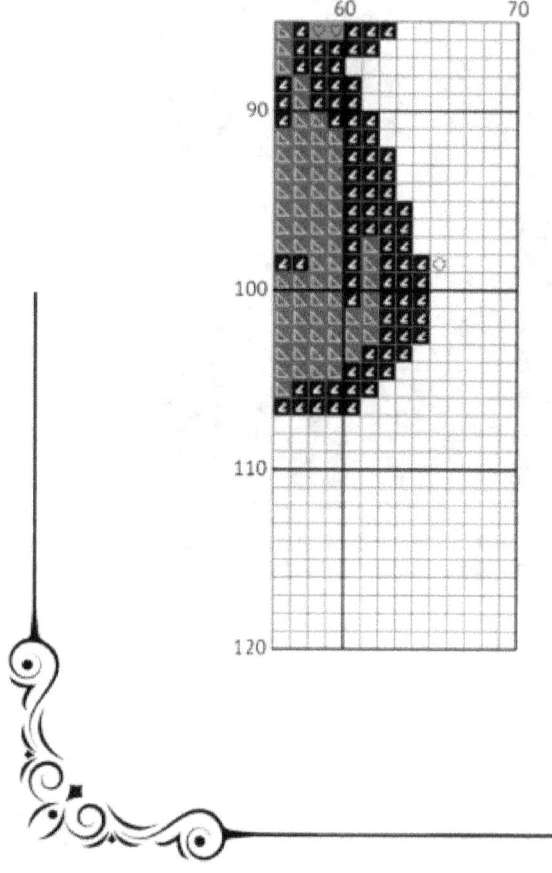

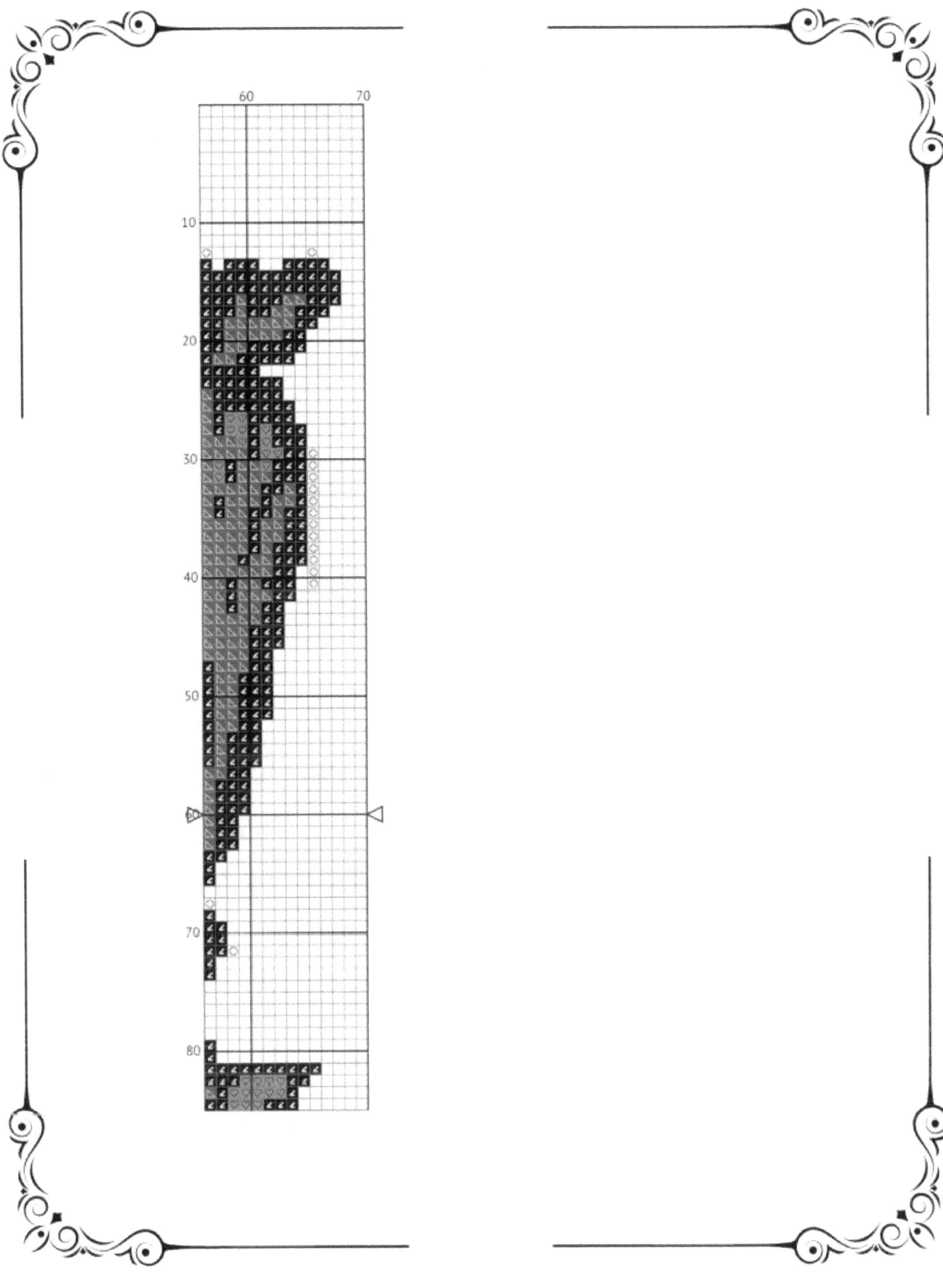

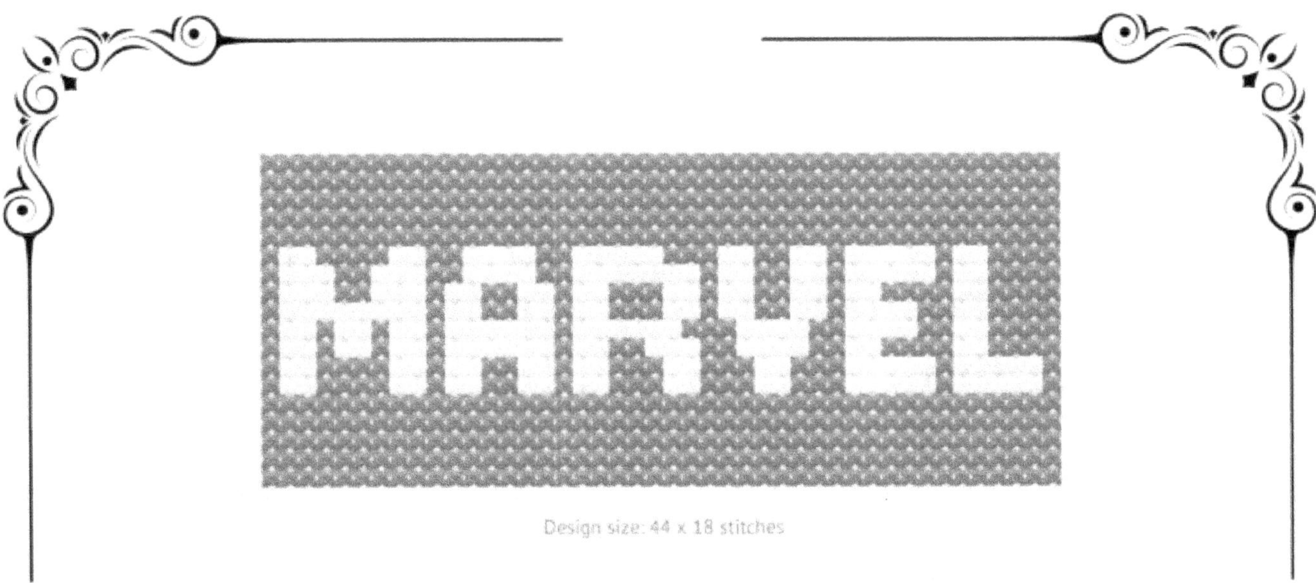

Design size: 44 x 18 stitches

Floss list for crosses

Use 2 strands of thread for cross stitch

N	Symbol		Number	Name	Stitches
1	∠	∠	DMC B5200	Snow White	201
2	☐	▣	DMC 351	Coral	591

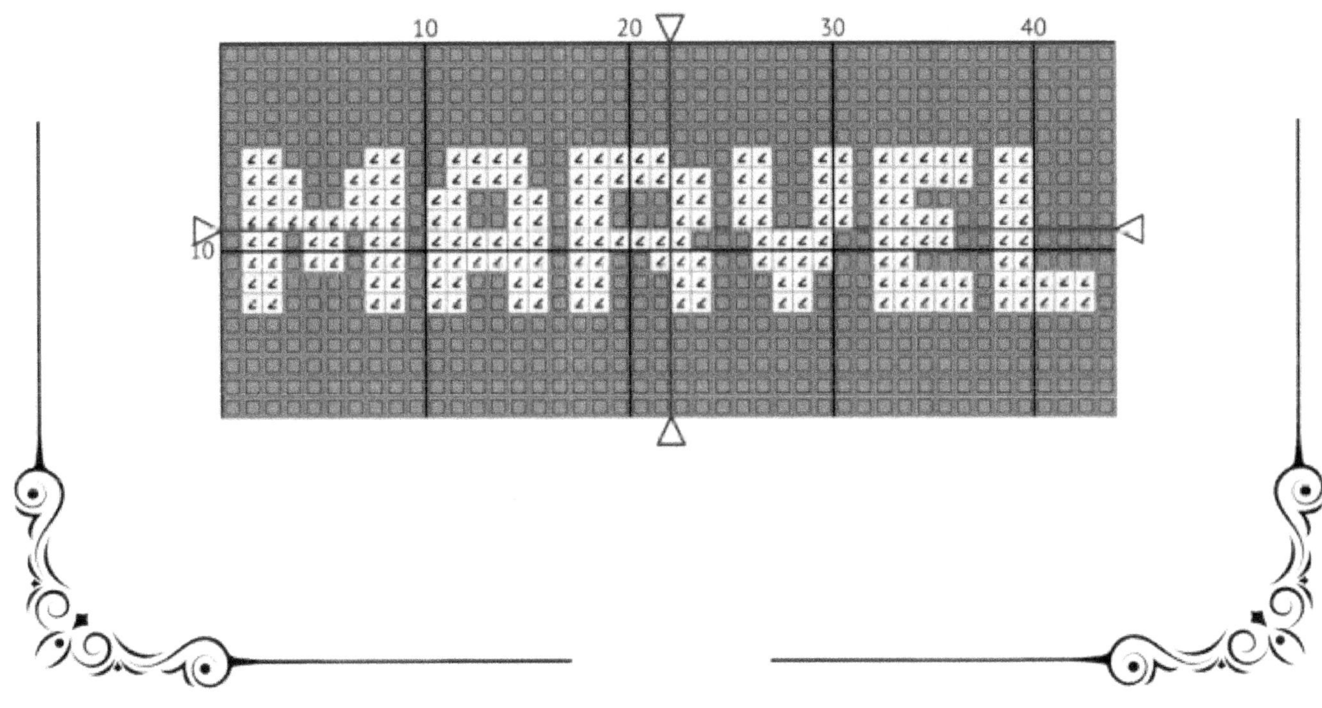

Design size: 100 x 51 stitches

Use 2 strands of thread for cross stitch

N	Symbol		Number	Name	Stitches
1	T	T	DMC B5200	Snow White	95
2	♡	♡	DMC 02	Tin	146
3	⚮	⚮	DMC 304	Red - Medium	96
4	●	○	DMC 310	Black	718
5	✳	✳	DMC 437	Tan - Light	41
6	■	■	DMC 645	Beaver Gray - Very Dark	151
7	☆	☆	DMC 666	Red - Bright	151
8	m	m	DMC 792	Cornflower Blue - Dark	135
9	=	=	DMC 816	Garnet	170
10	//	//	DMC 900	Burnt Orange - Dark	70
11	◇	◇	DMC 902	Garnet - Very Dark	219
12	✛	✛	DMC 924	Gray Green - Very Dark	83
13	✂	✂	DMC 964	Seagreen - Light	10
14	<	<	DMC 967	Apricot - Very Light	58
15	⌐	⌐	DMC 973	Canary - Bright	58
16	○	○	DMC 995	Electric Blue - Dark	159
17	◁	◁	DMC 3022	Brown Gray - Medium	114
18	▽	▽	DMC 3753	Antique Blue - Ultra Very Light	34
19	7	7	DMC 3821	Straw	71
20	S	S	DMC 3826	Golden Brown	25

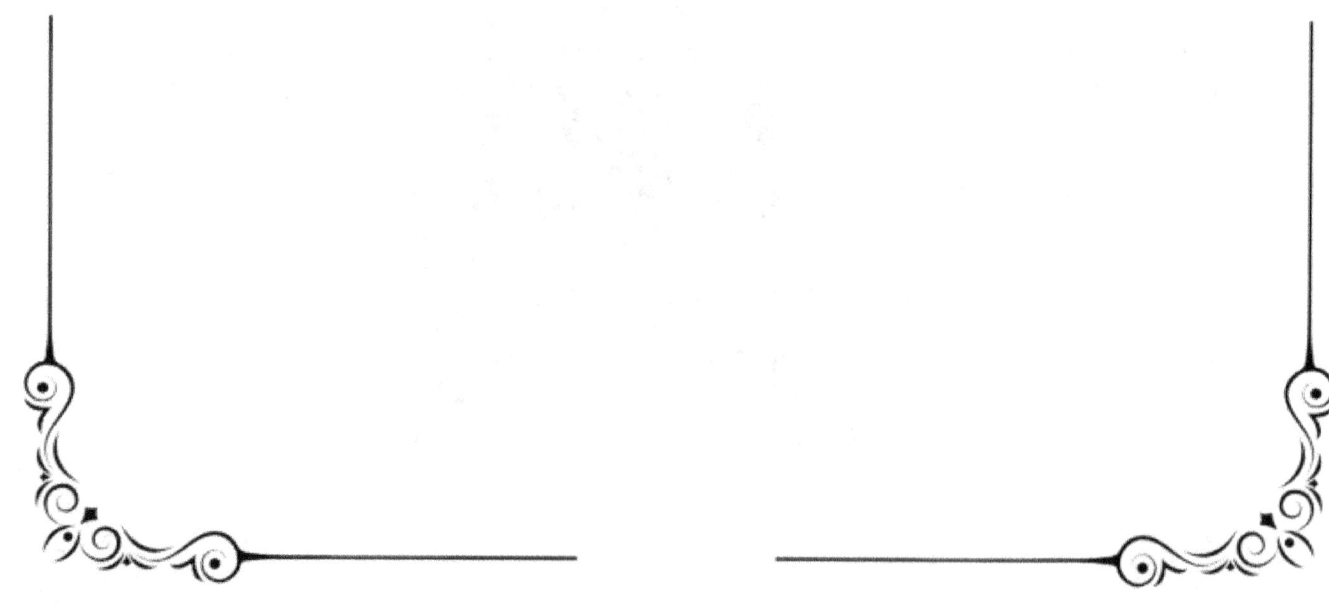

Design size: 50 x 50 stitches

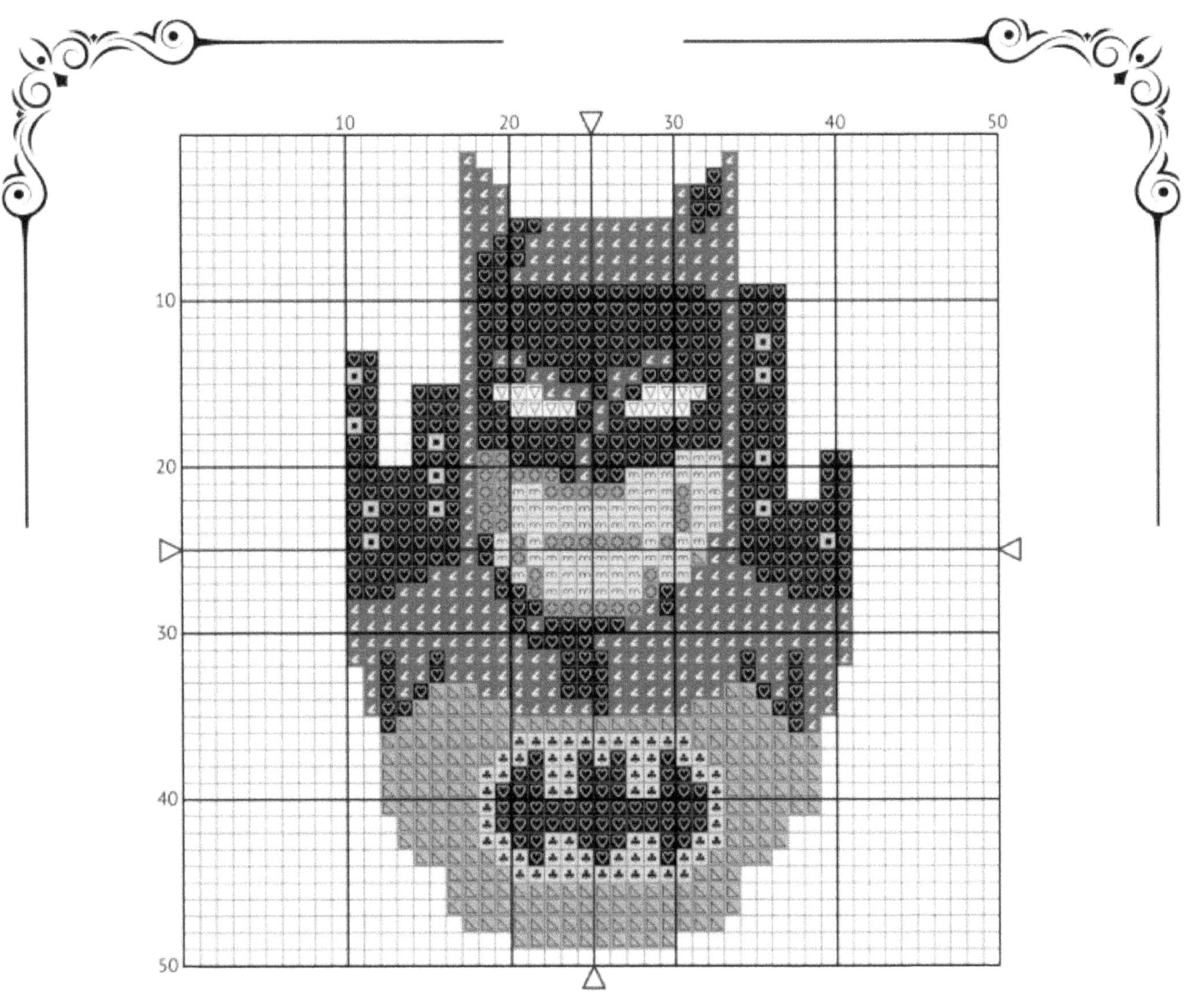

Floss list for crosses

Use 2 strands of thread for cross stitch

N	Symbol		Number	Name	Stitches
1	▽	▽	DMC B5200	Snow White	15
2	■	■	DMC 16	Chartreuse - Light	12
3	♡	♥	DMC 310	Black	399
4	♣	♣	DMC 444	Lemon - Dark	67
5	◁	◁	DMC 927	Gray Green - Light	203
6	m	m	DMC 950	Desert Sand - Light	71
7	✤	✤	DMC 3045	Yellow Beige - Dark	40
8	◢	◢	DMC 3768	Gray Green - Dark	299

Design size: 50 x 59 stitches

Floss list for crosses

Use 2 strands of thread for cross stitch

N	Symbol		Number	Name	Stitches
1	♣	♣	DMC B5200	Snow White	52
2	●	●	DMC 334	Baby Blue - Medium	322
3	♡	♡	DMC 813	Blue - Light	191
4	▽	▽	DMC 839	Beige Brown - Dark	205
5	■	■	DMC 840	Beige Brown - Medium	302
6	◺	◺	DMC 924	Gray Green - Very Dark	122
7	◢	◢	DMC 930	Antique Blue - Dark	350
8	☆	☆	DMC 3688	Mauve - Medium	10
9	m	m	DMC 3747	Blue Violet - Very Light	26
10	◦	◦	DMC 3770	Tawny - Very Light	181
11	✛	✛	DMC 3864	Mocha Beige - Light	201

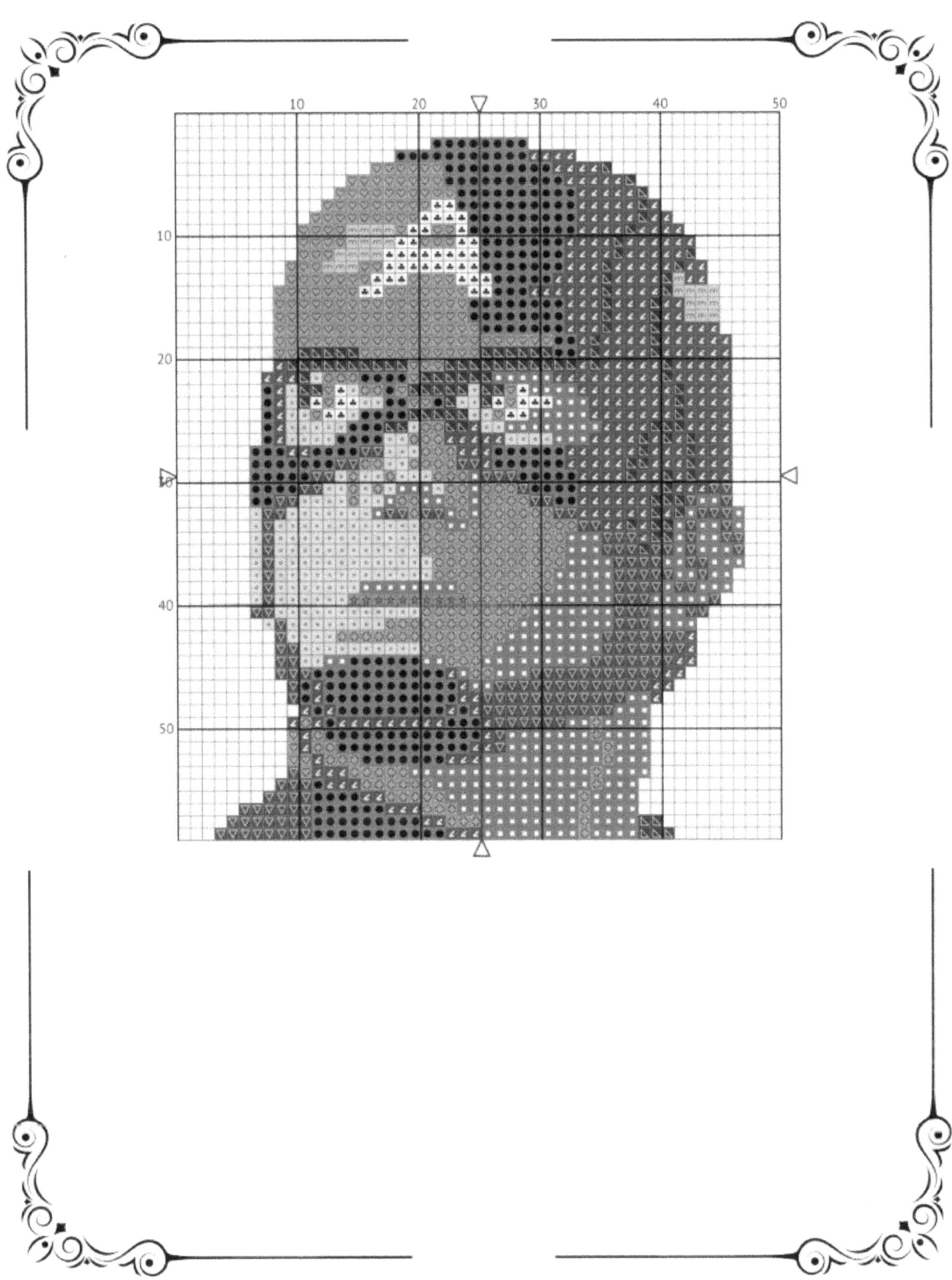

Design size: 70 x 67 stitches

Floss list for crosses

Use 2 strands of thread for cross stitch

N	Symbol		Number	Name	Stitches
1	■	■	DMC B5200	Snow White	6
2	♣	♣	DMC 22	Alizarin	845
3	m	m	DMC 310	Black	1143
4	◺	◺	DMC 535	Ash Gray - Very Light	43

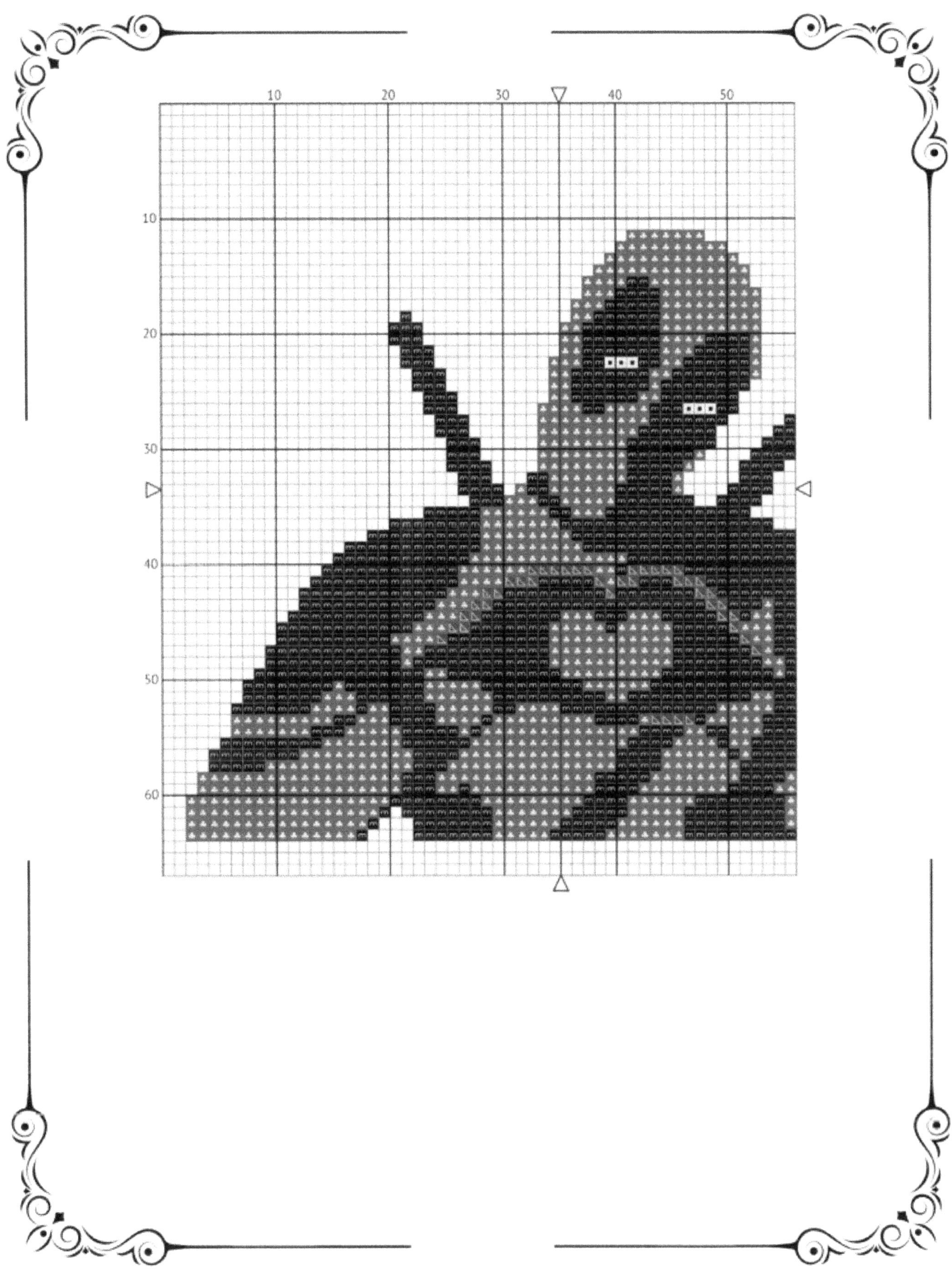

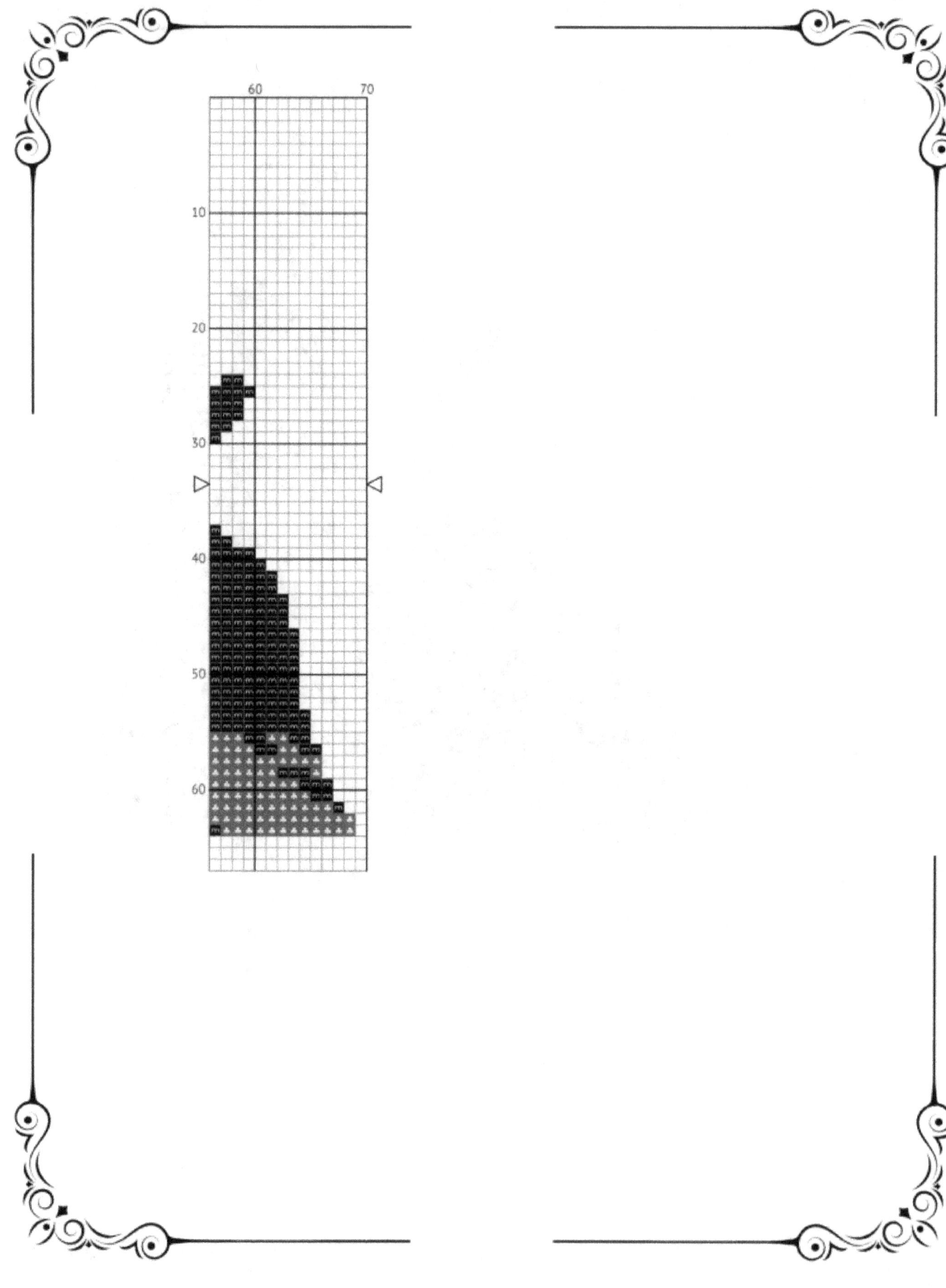

Design size: 40 x 60 stitches

Floss list for crosses

Use 2 strands of thread for cross stitch

N	Symbol		Number	Name	Stitches
1	≡	≡	DMC B5200	Snow White	25
2	☐	☐	DMC 304	Red - Medium	731
3	■	☐	DMC 310	Black	2
4	♡	♥	DMC 814	Garnet - Dark	315
5	◢	◢	DMC 961	Seagreen - Light	501
6	♣	♣	DMC 3823	Yellow - Ultra Pale	315
7	◺	◺	DMC 3842	Wedgwood - Very Dark	513

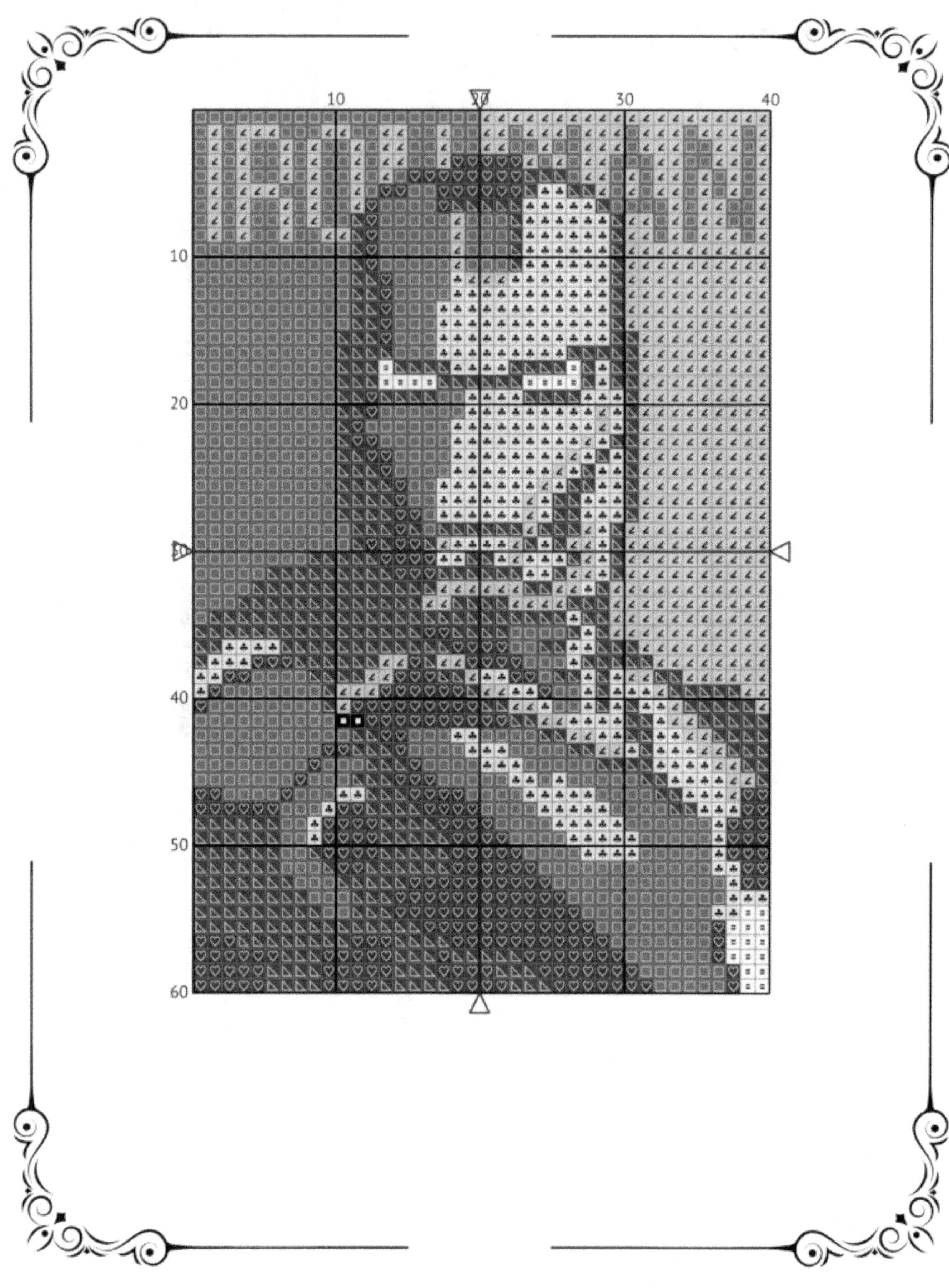

MARVEL

Design size: 50 x 50 stitches

Floss list for crosses

Use 2 strands of thread for cross stitch

N	Symbol		Number	Name	Stitches
1	m	m	DMC B5200	Snow White	527
2	∠	∠	DMC 16	Chartreuse - Light	35
3	#	#	DMC 321	Red	13
4	♣	♣	DMC 543	Beige - Ultra Very Light	84
5	◊	◊	DMC 552	Violet - Medium	203
6	✕	✕	DMC 794	Cornflower Blue - Light	84
7	‹	‹	DMC 825	Blue - Dark	113
8	□	□	DMC 905	Parrot Green - Dark	146
9	○	○	DMC 912	Emerald Green - Light	66
10	⌐	⌐	DMC 915	Plum - Dark	86
11	●	○	DMC 934	Avocado Green - Black	593
12	◺	◺	DMC 3747	Blue Violet - Very Light	550

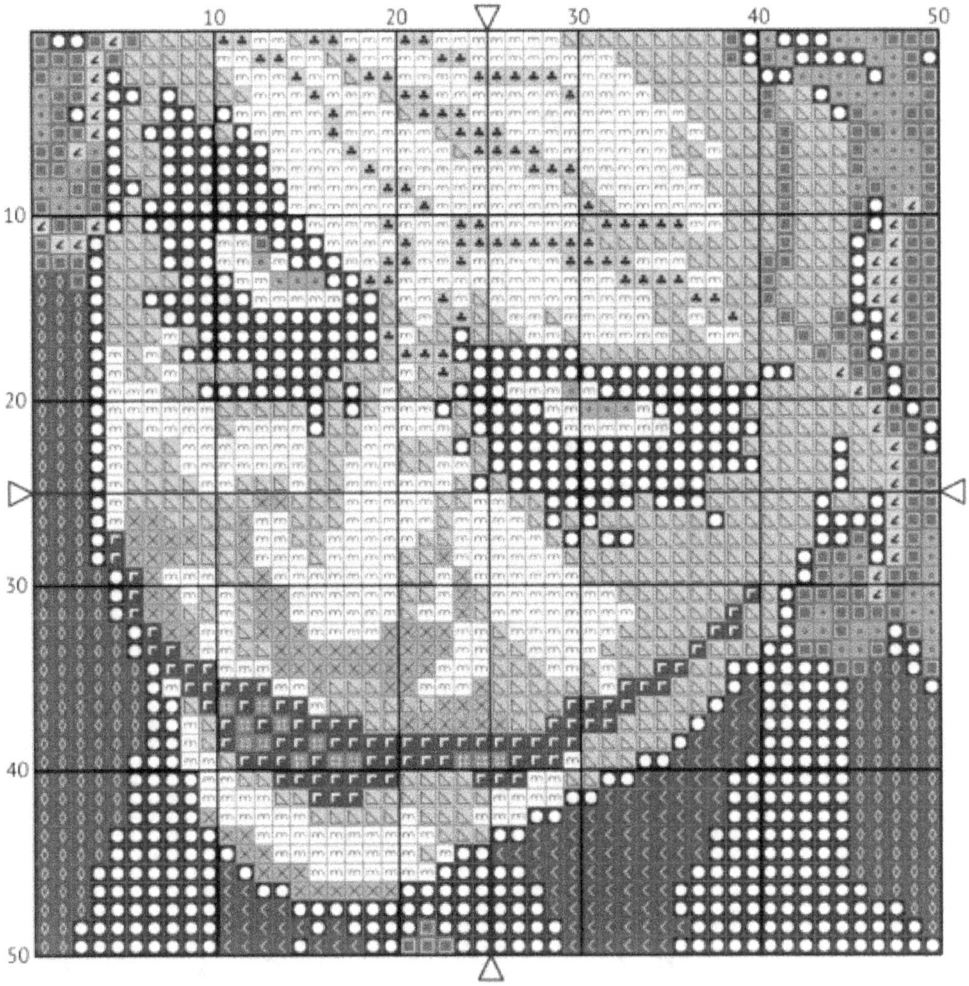
10
20
30
40
50
10
20
30
40
50

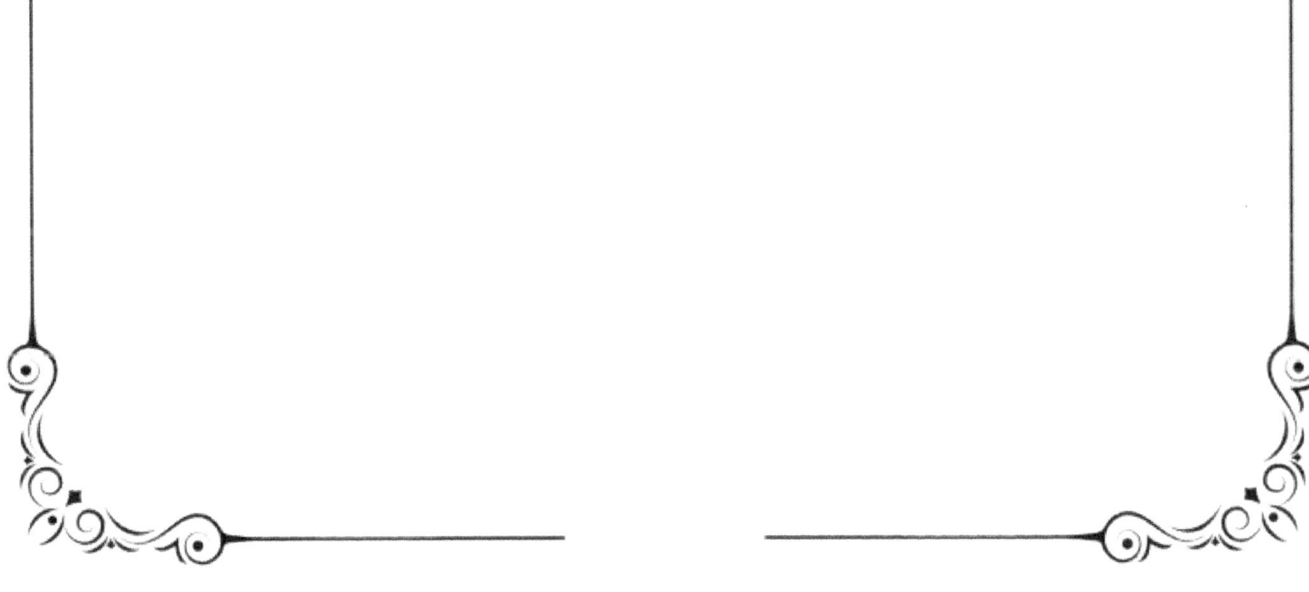

Design size: 90 x 126 stitches

Floss list for crosses

Use 2 strands of thread for cross stitch

N	Symbol		Number	Name	Stitches
1	>	>	DMC 307	Lemon	1198
2	<	<	DMC 310	Black	1399
3	⌐	⌐	DMC 796	Royal Blue - Dark	1746
4	✦	✿	DMC 829	Golden Olive - Very Dark	398
5	↑	↑	DMC 832	Golden Olive	688
6	⚊	⚊	DMC 834	Golden Olive - Very Light	899
7	(	(	DMC 3811	Turquoise - Very Light	540
8	✳	✳	DMC 3843	Electric Blue	1001
9	m	m	DMC BLANK	White	896

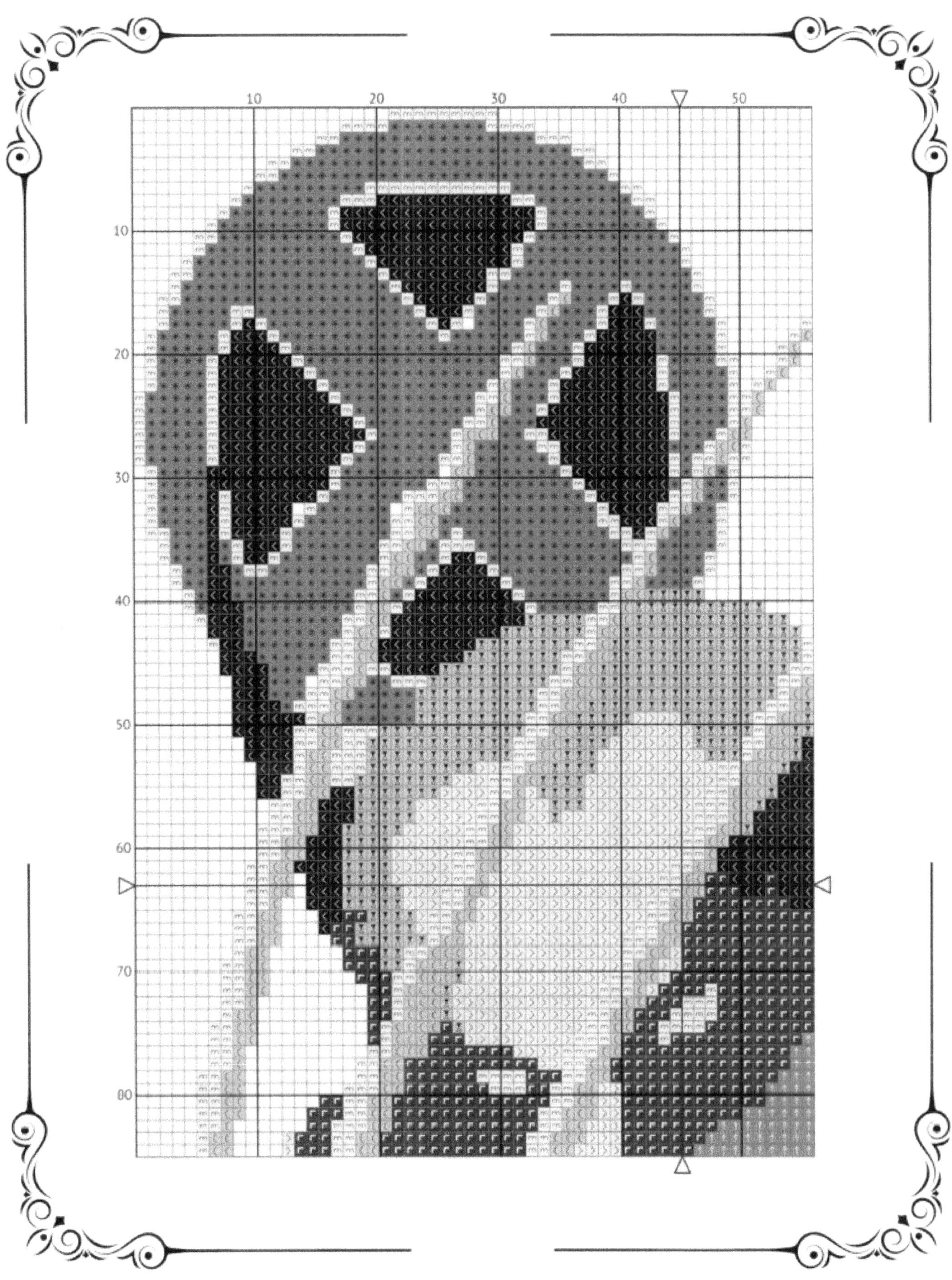

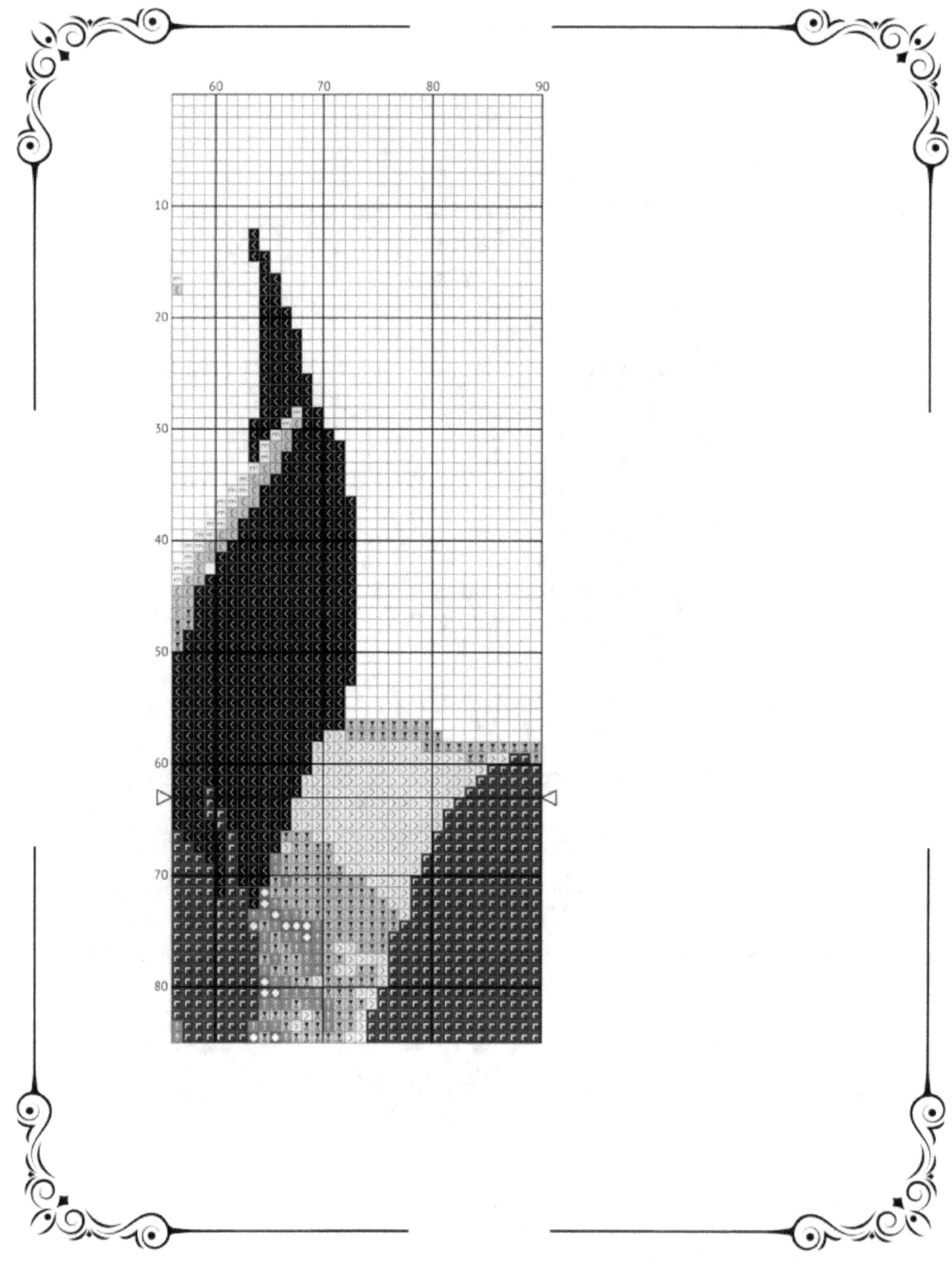

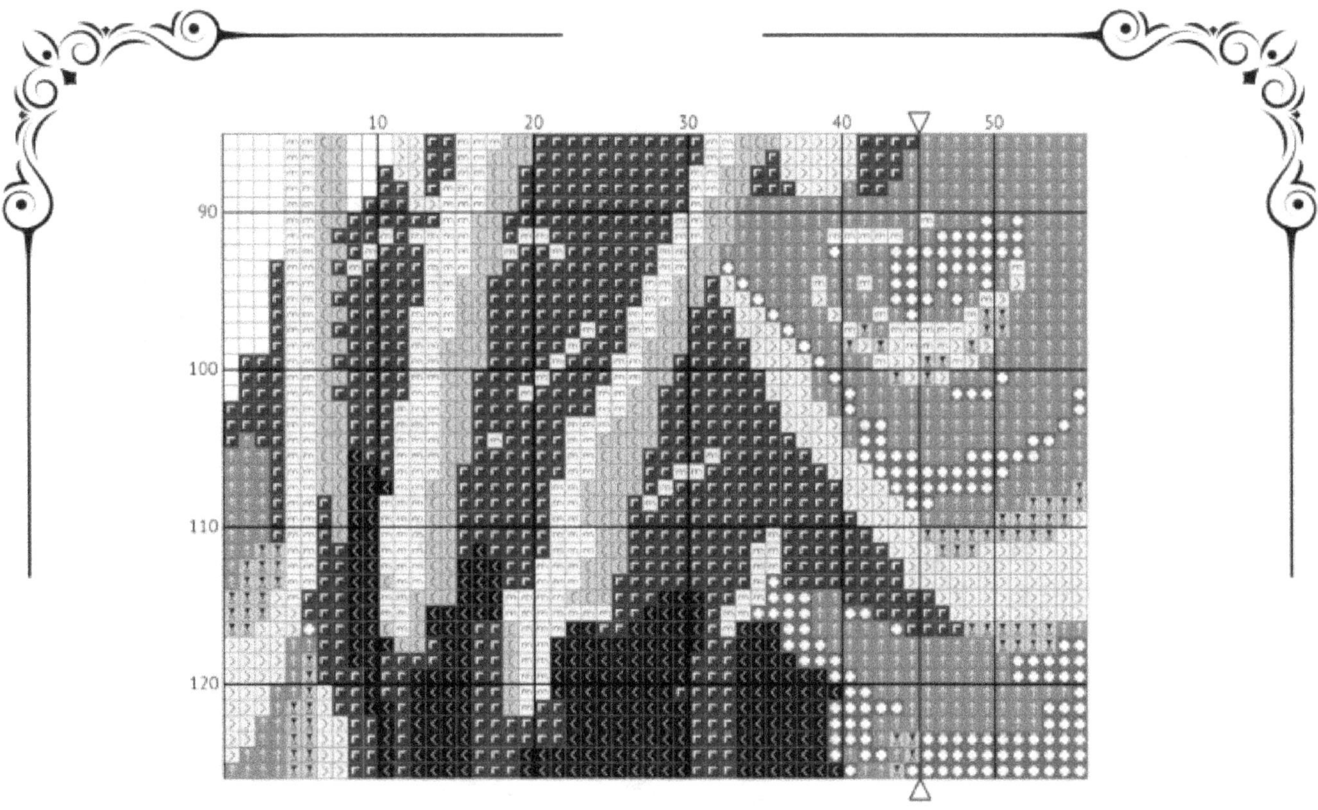

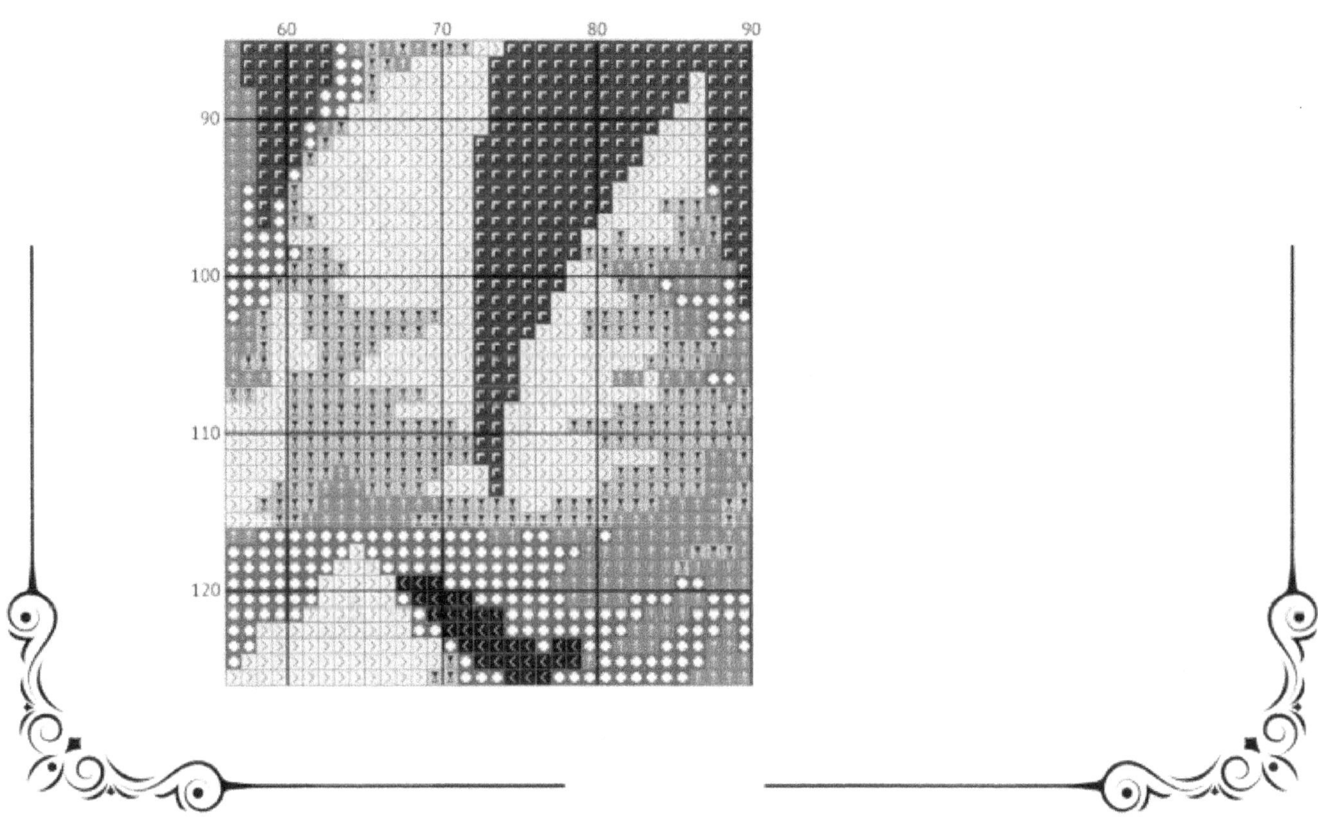

Design size: 104 x 77 stitches

Floss list for crosses

Use 2 strands of thread for cross stitch

N	Symbol		Number	Name	Stitches
1	■	■	DMC 307	Lemon	431
2	◦	◦	DMC 310	Black	1167
3	✛	✛	DMC 666	Red - Bright	1009
4	m	m	DMC 702	Kelly Green	364
5	☆	☆	DMC 825	Blue - Dark	295
6	●	●	DMC B5200	Snow White	748

Use 1 strand of thread for backstitch

N	Line style	Number	Name	Units
1	————	DMC 310	Black	84

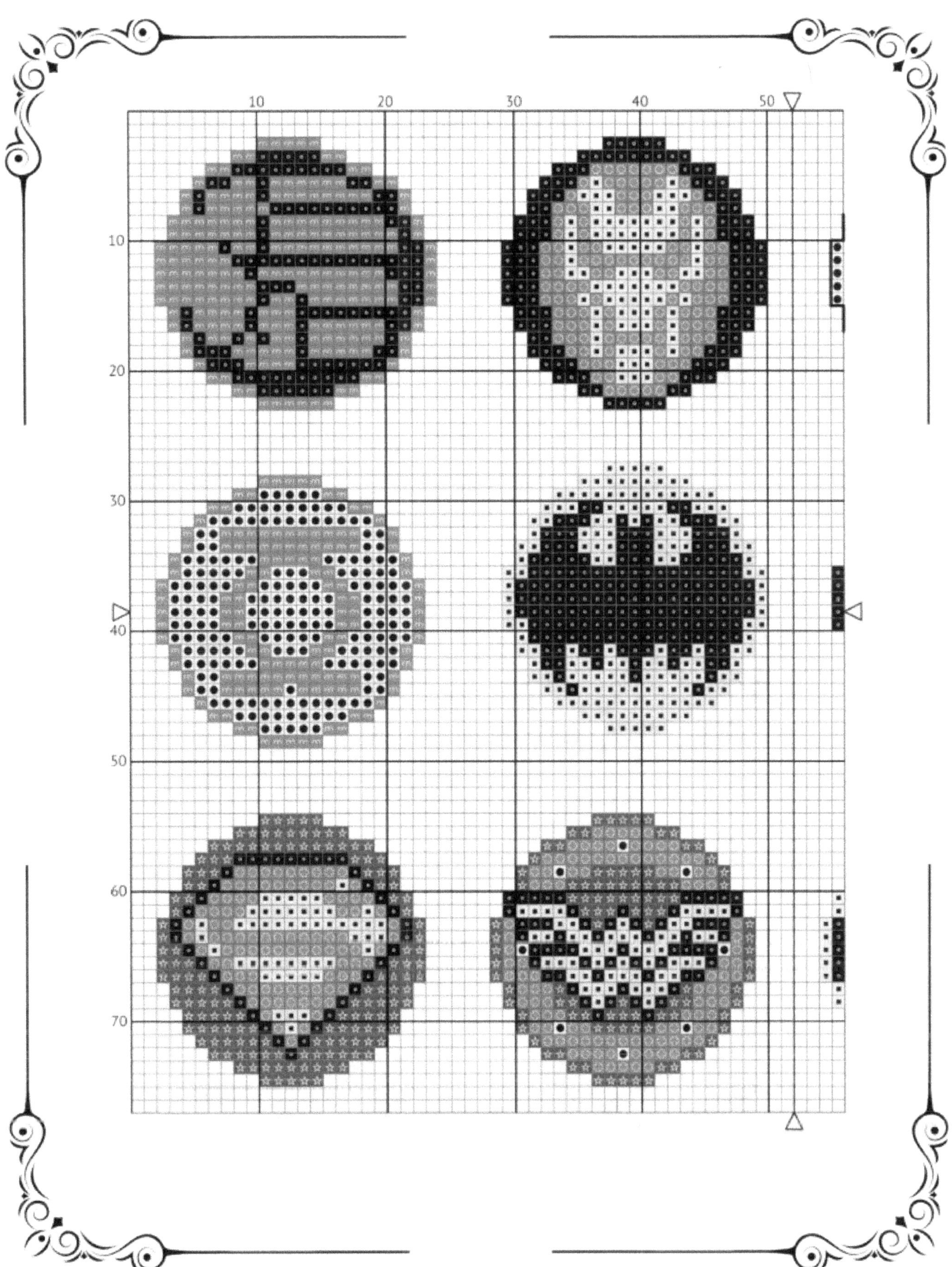

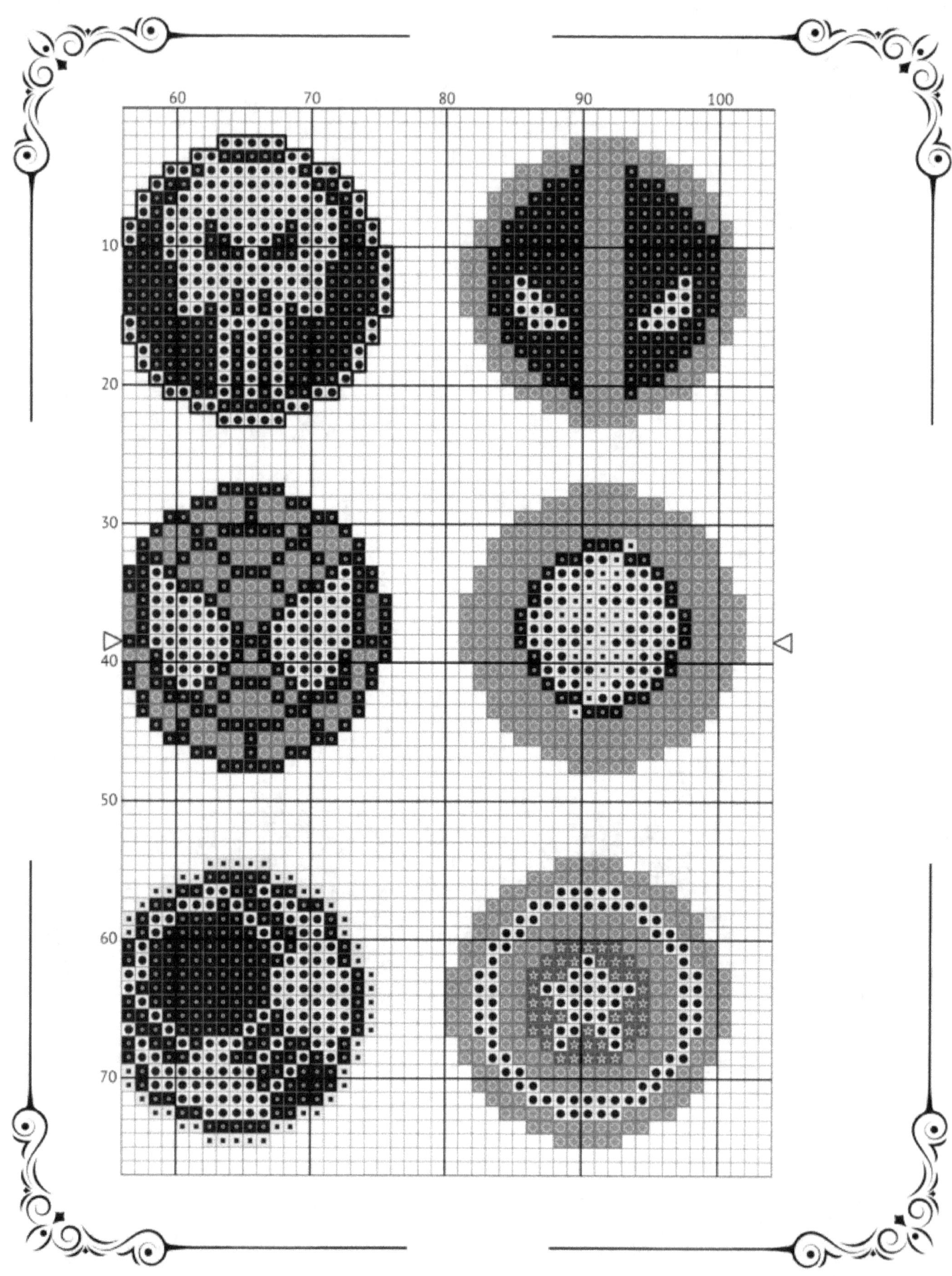

Design size: 111 x 220 stitches

Floss list for crosses

Use 2 strands of thread for cross stitch

N	Symbol		Number	Name	Stitches
1	■	■	DMC 307	Lemon	147
2	▽	▽	DMC 798	Delft Blue - Dark	147
3	m	m	DMC 900	Burnt Orange - Dark	147
4	✿	✿	DMC 946	Burnt Orange - Medium	147
5	♣	♣	DMC 3688	Mauve - Medium	147
6	●	○	DMC 3799	Pewter Gray - Very Dark	8493
7	◦	◦	DMC 3850	Bright Green - Dark	147

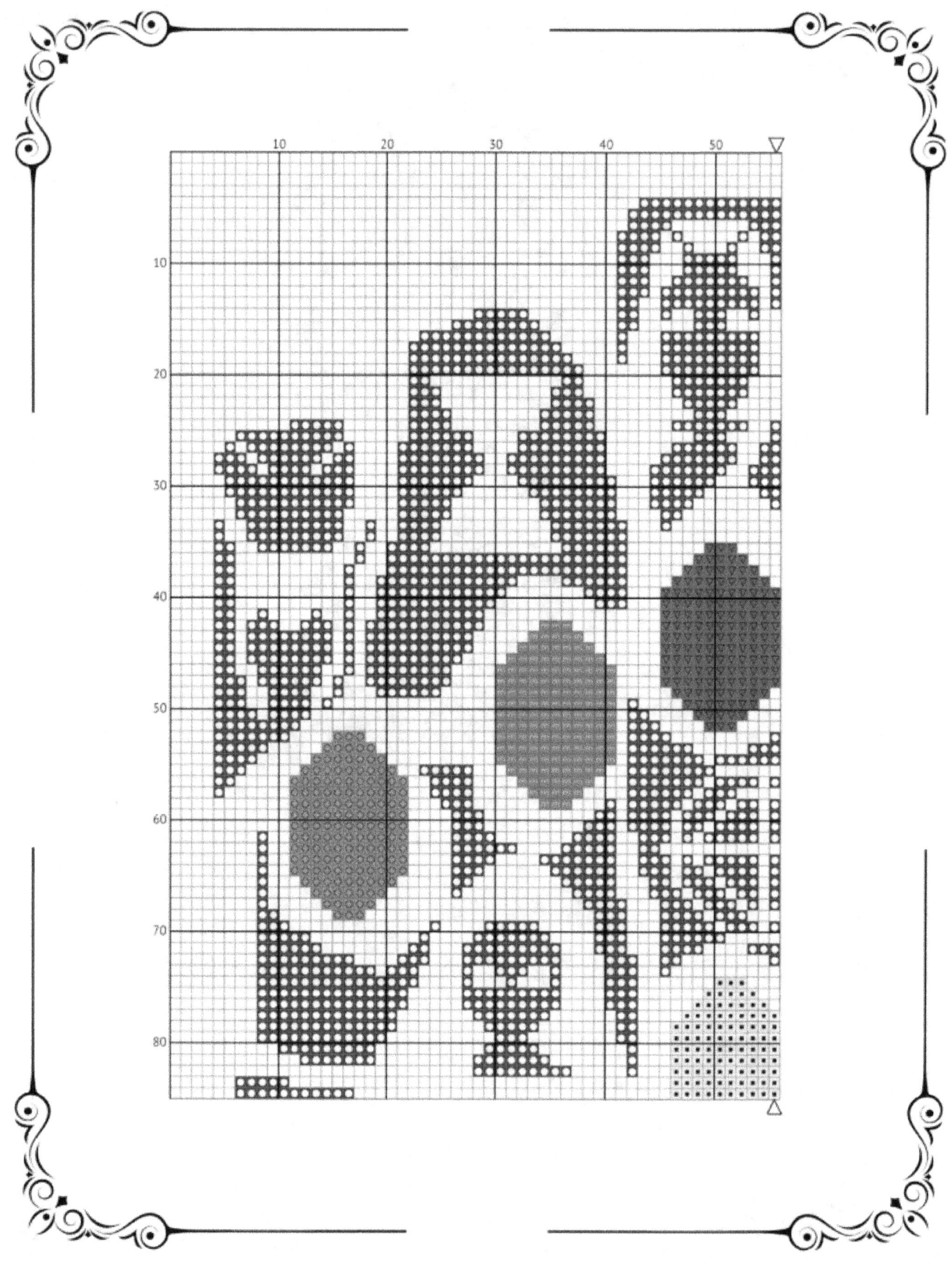

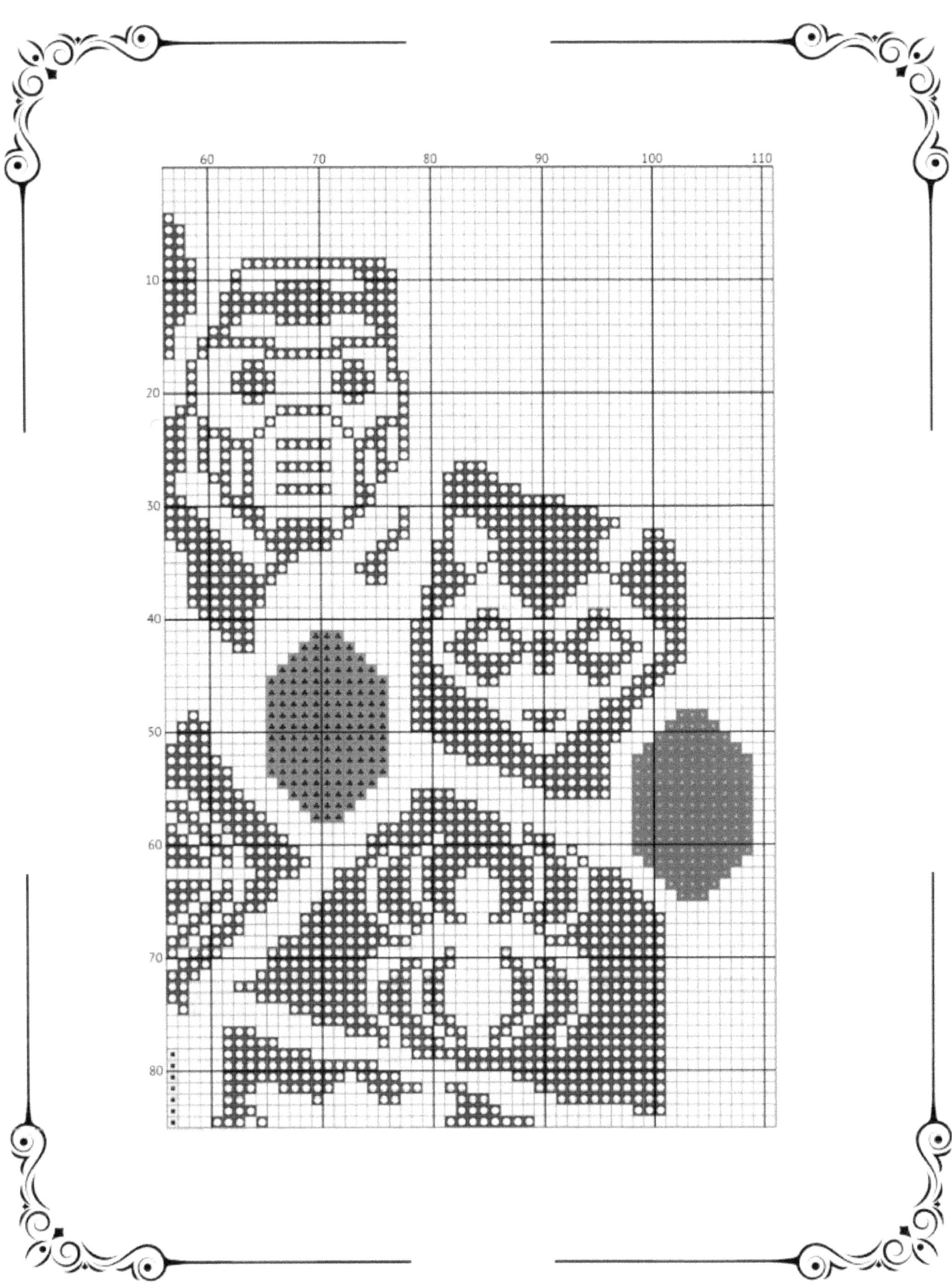

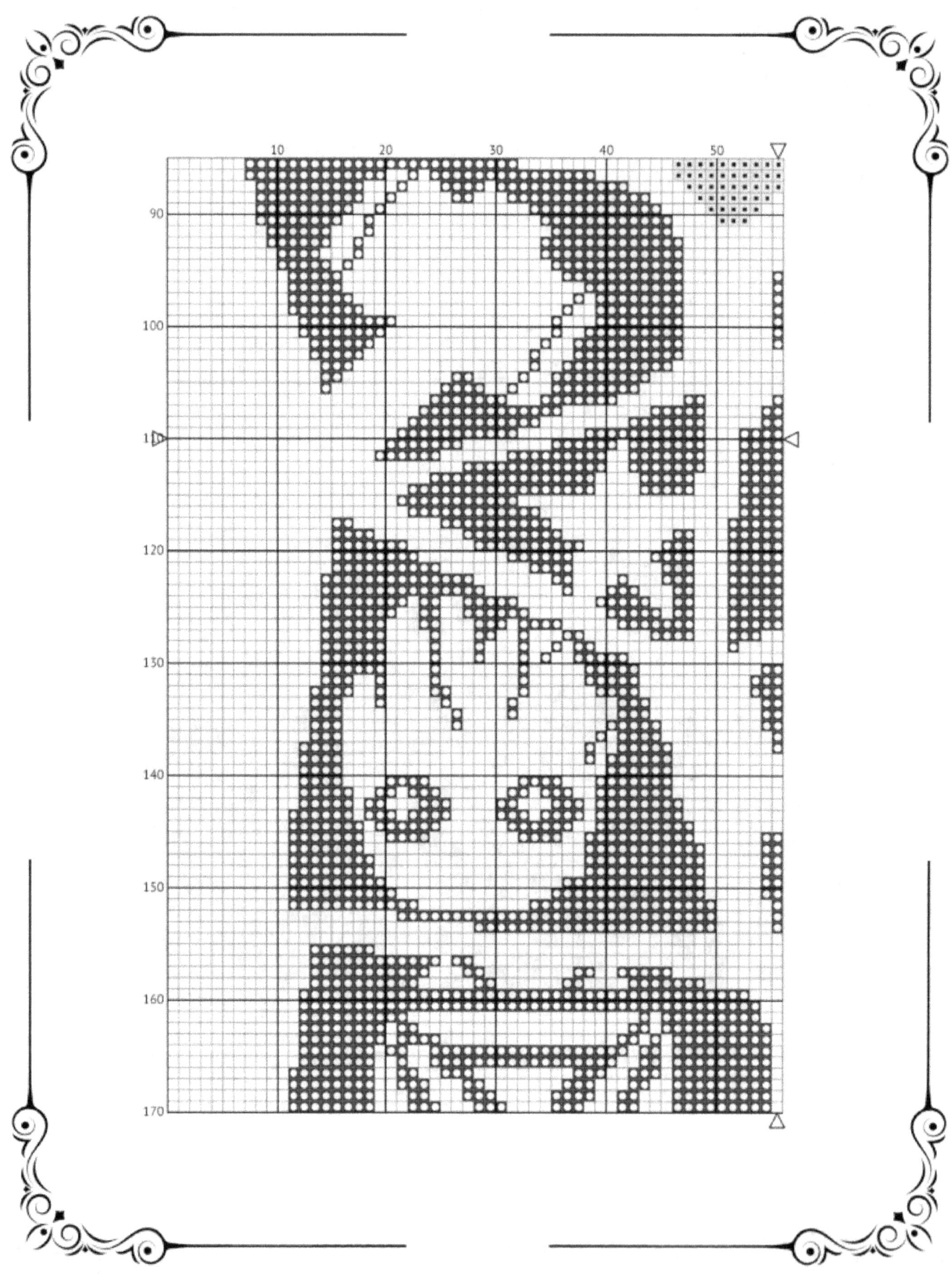

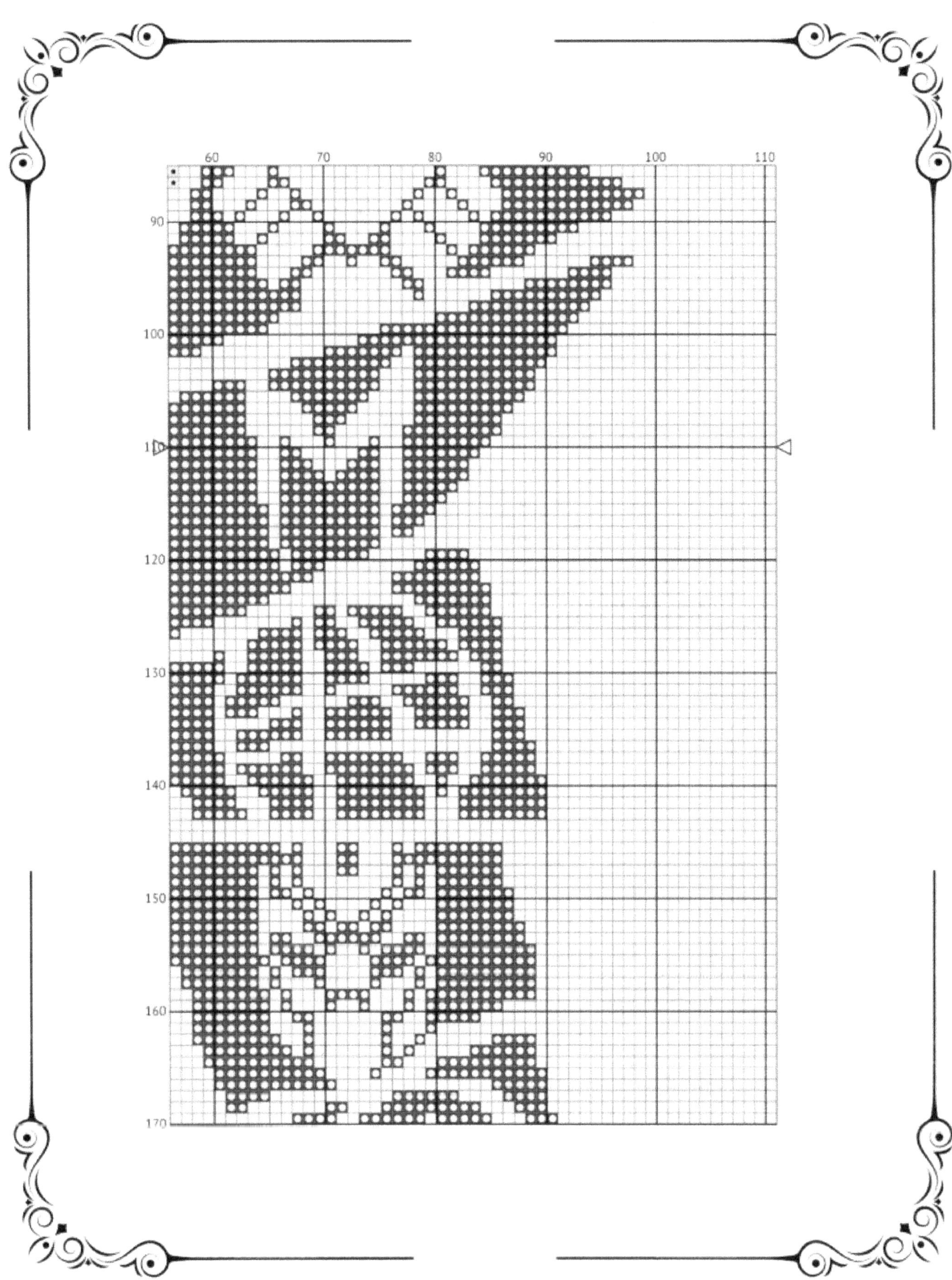

10
20
30
40
50
170
180
190
200
210
220

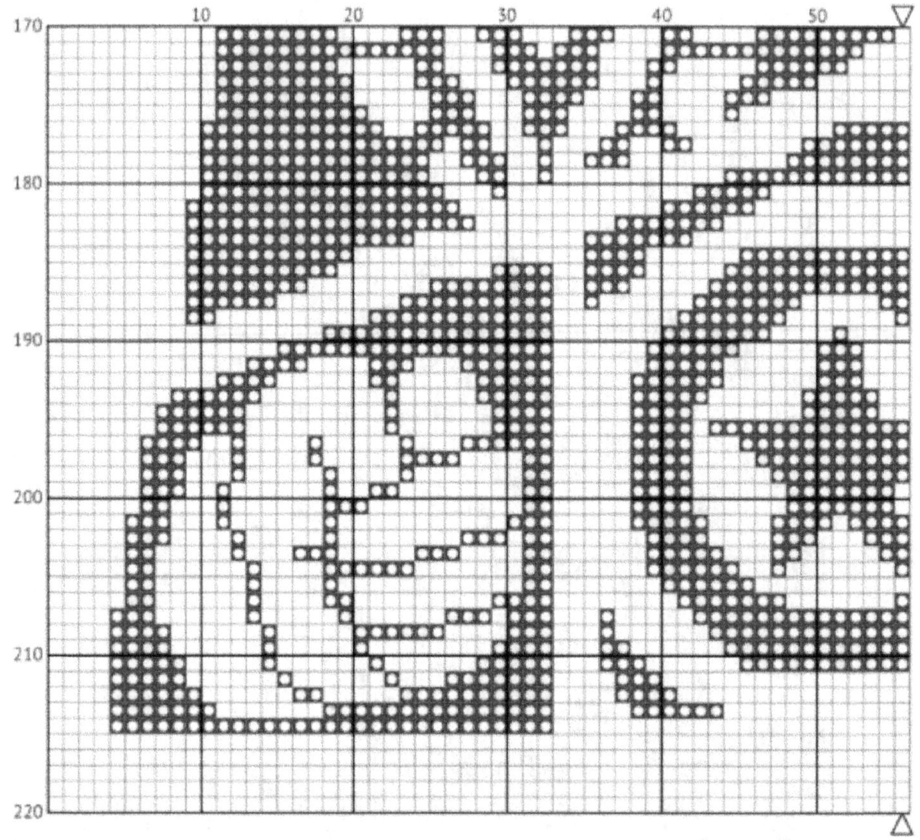

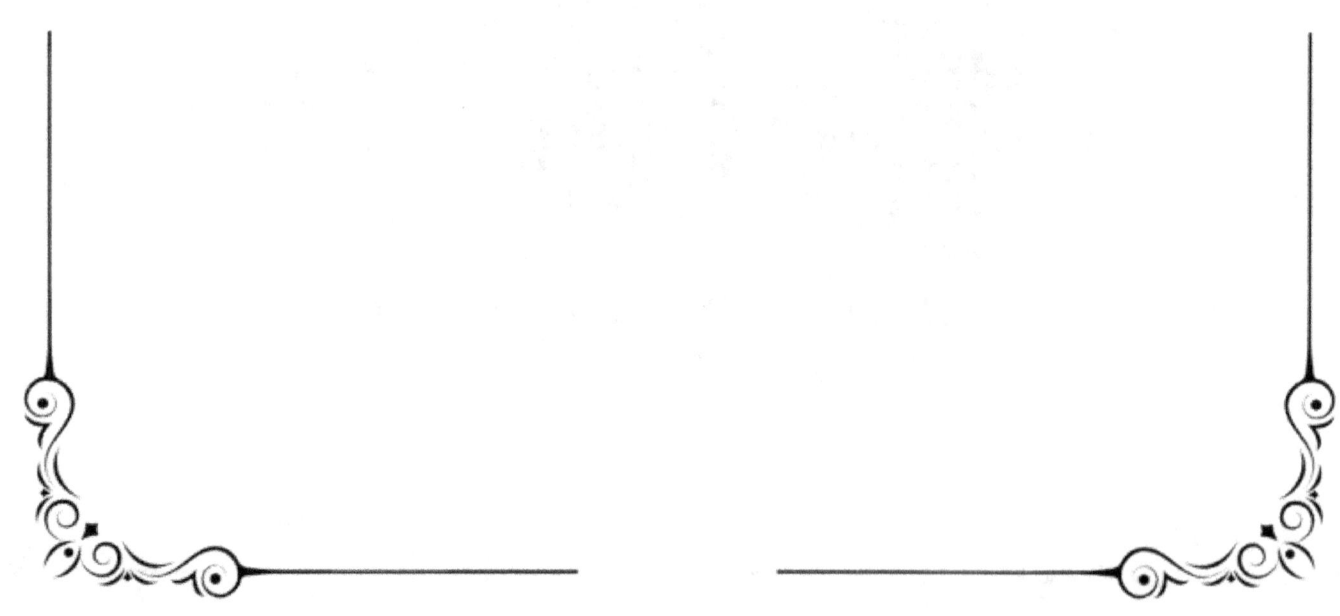

60
70
80
90
100
110
170
180
190
200
210
220

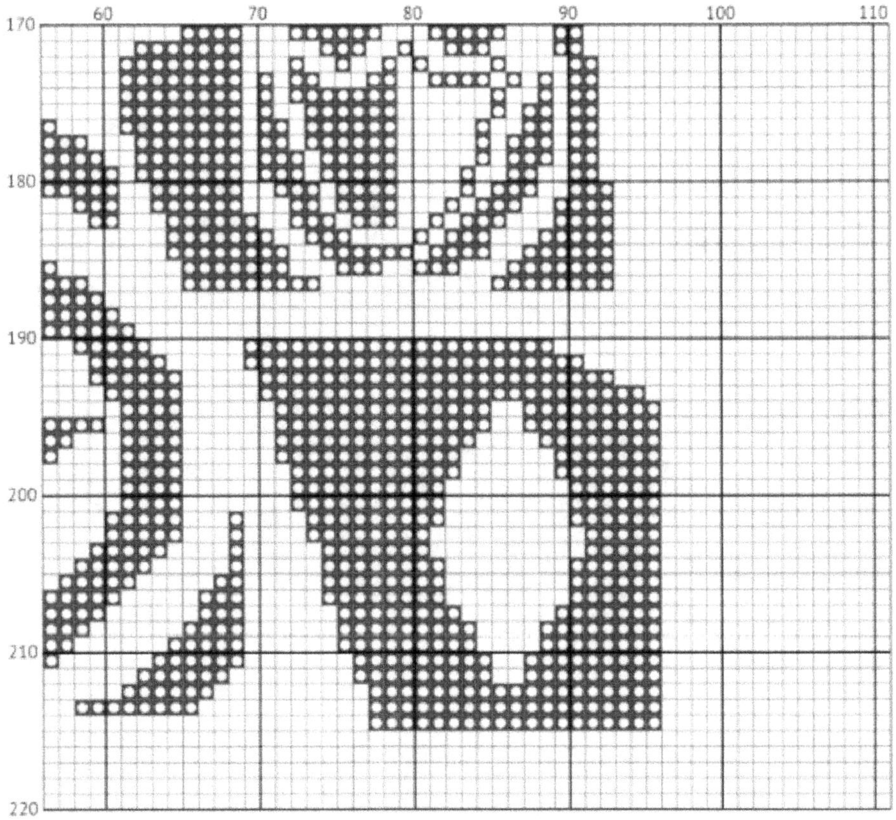

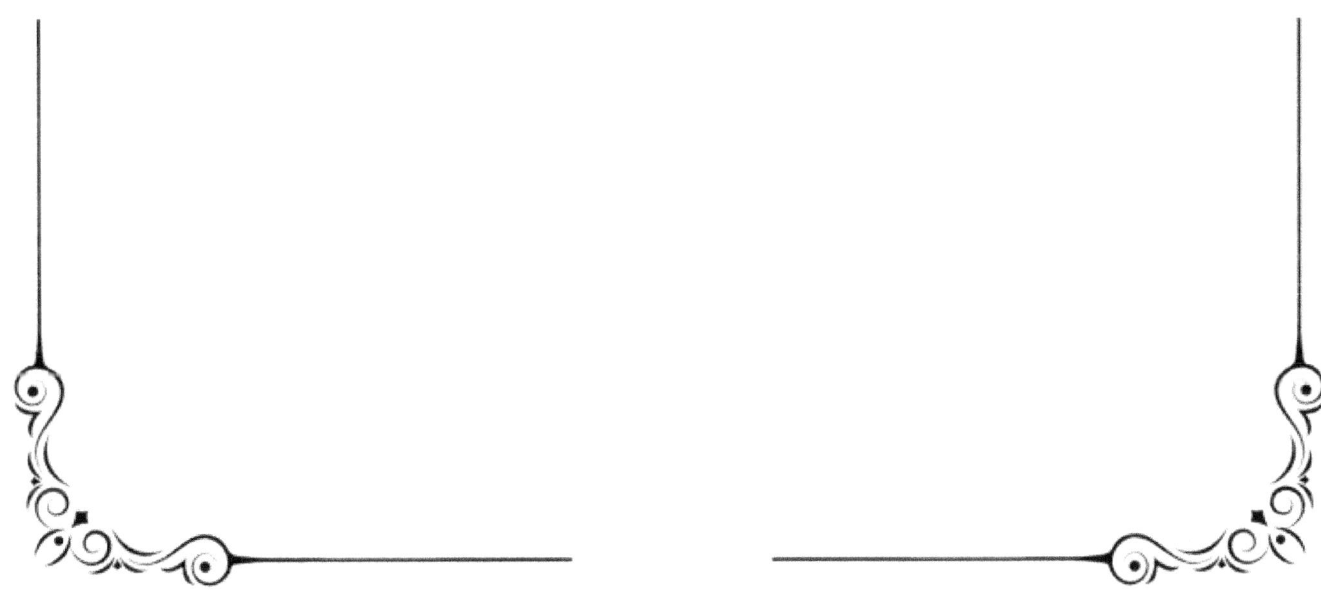

Design size: 55 x 63 stitches

Floss list for crosses

Use 2 strands of thread for cross stitch

N	Symbol		Number	Name	Stitches
1	○	○	DMC B5200	Snow White	16
2	◢	◢	DMC 161	Gray Blue	557
3	m	m	DMC 310	Black	190
4	♣	♣	DMC 720	Orange Spice - Dark	558
5	♡	♡	DMC 816	Garnet	310

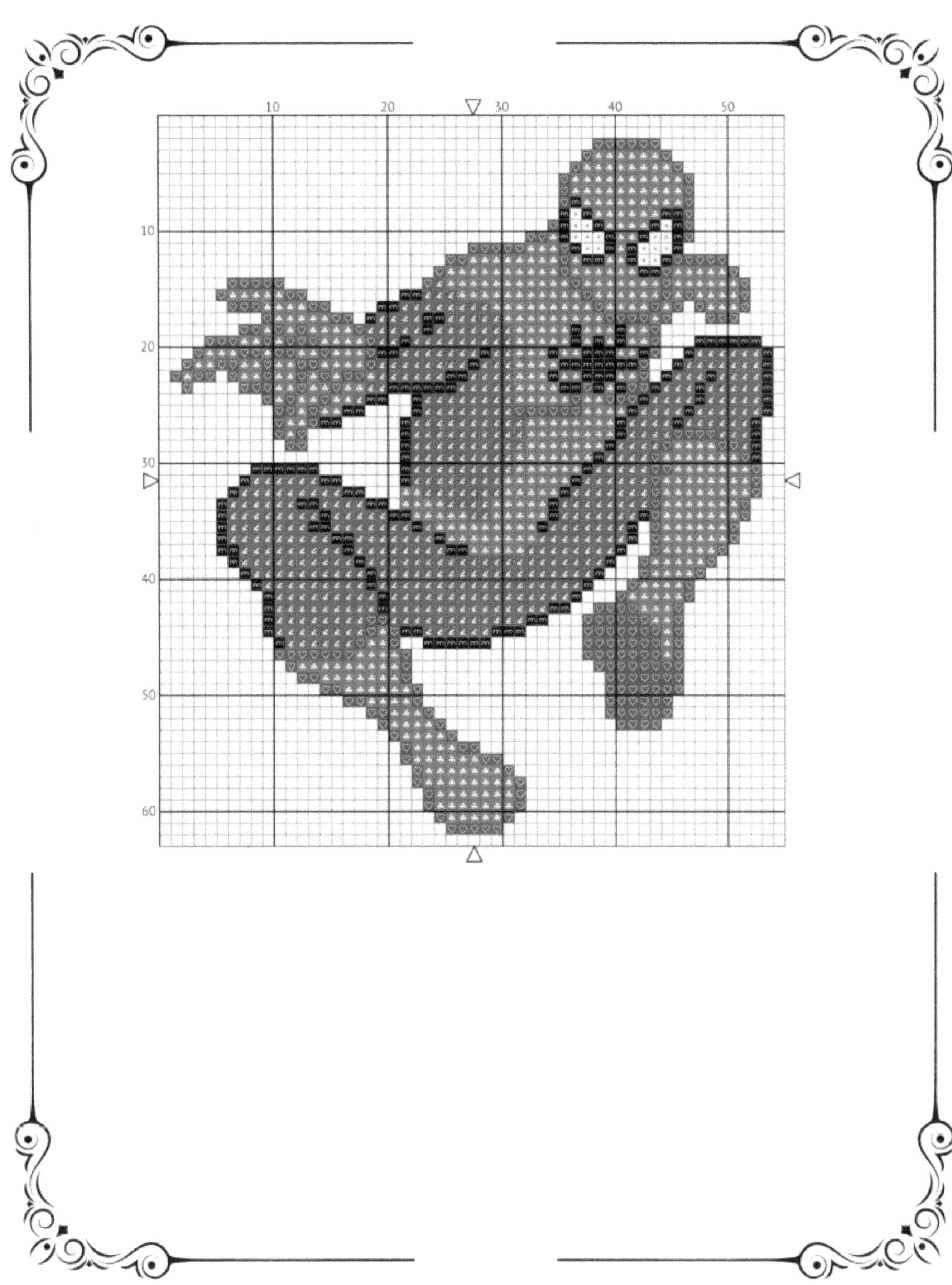

Design size: 100 x 100 stitches

Floss list for crosses

Use 2 strands of thread for cross stitch

N	Symbol		Number	Name	Stitches
1			DMC 06	Driftwood - Medium Light	120
2			DMC 304	Red - Medium	752
3			DMC 744	Yellow - Pale	313
4			DMC 807	Peacock Blue	1025
5			DMC 816	Garnet	340
6			DMC 945	Tawny	83
7			DMC 950	Desert Sand - Light	629
8			DMC 3810	Turquoise - Dark	790
9			DMC B5200	Snow White	202
10			DMC 310	Black	2214

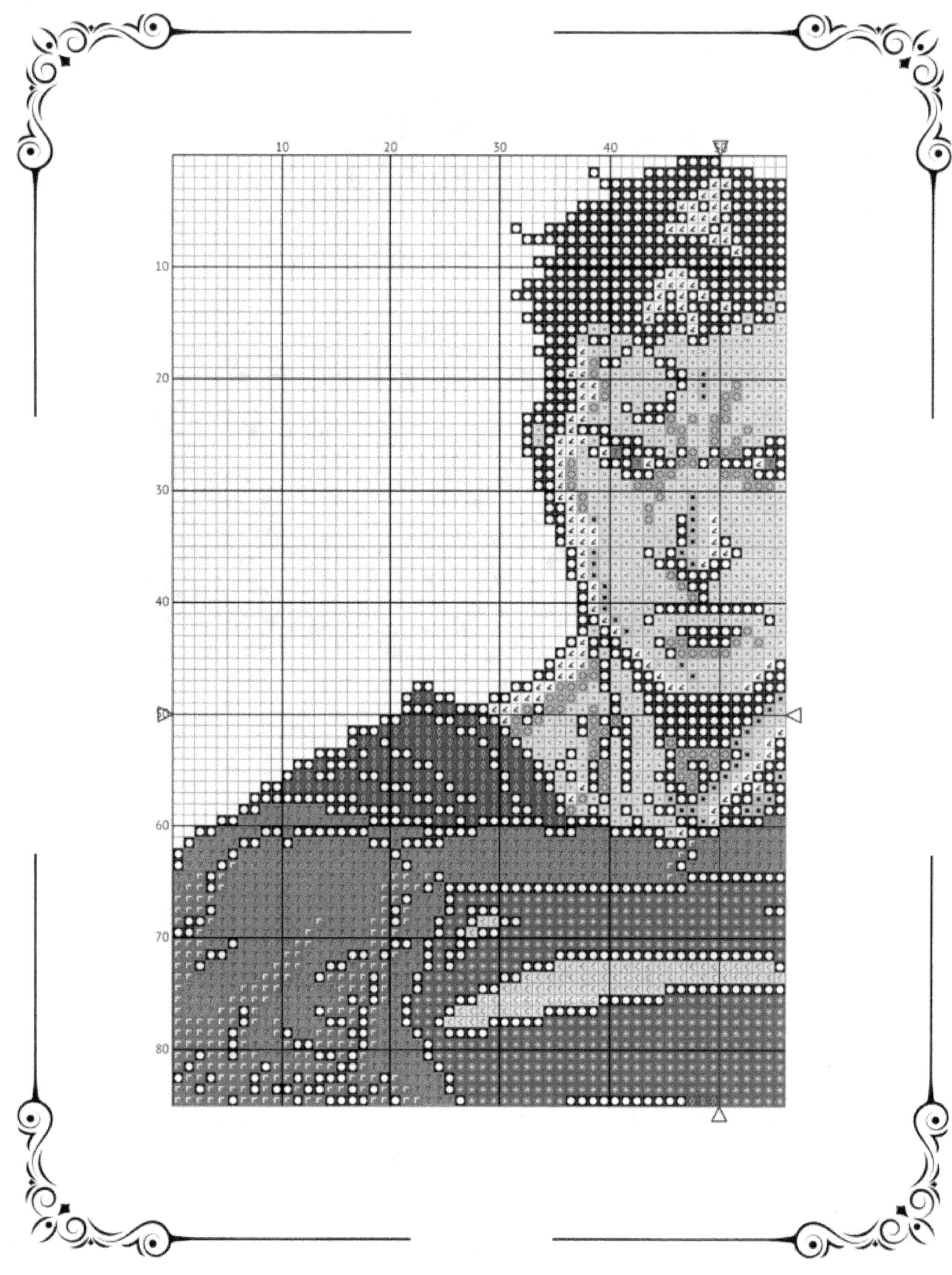

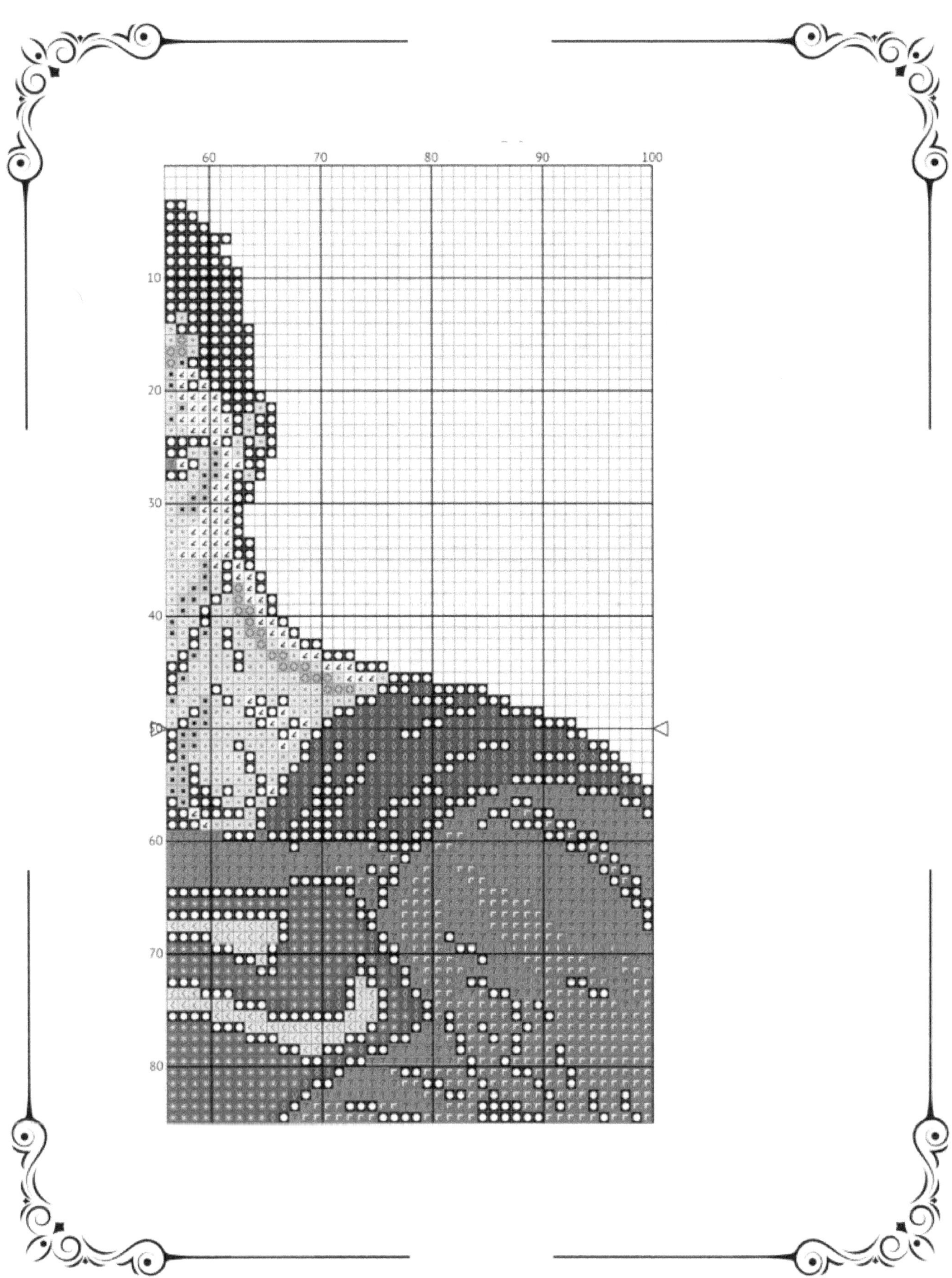

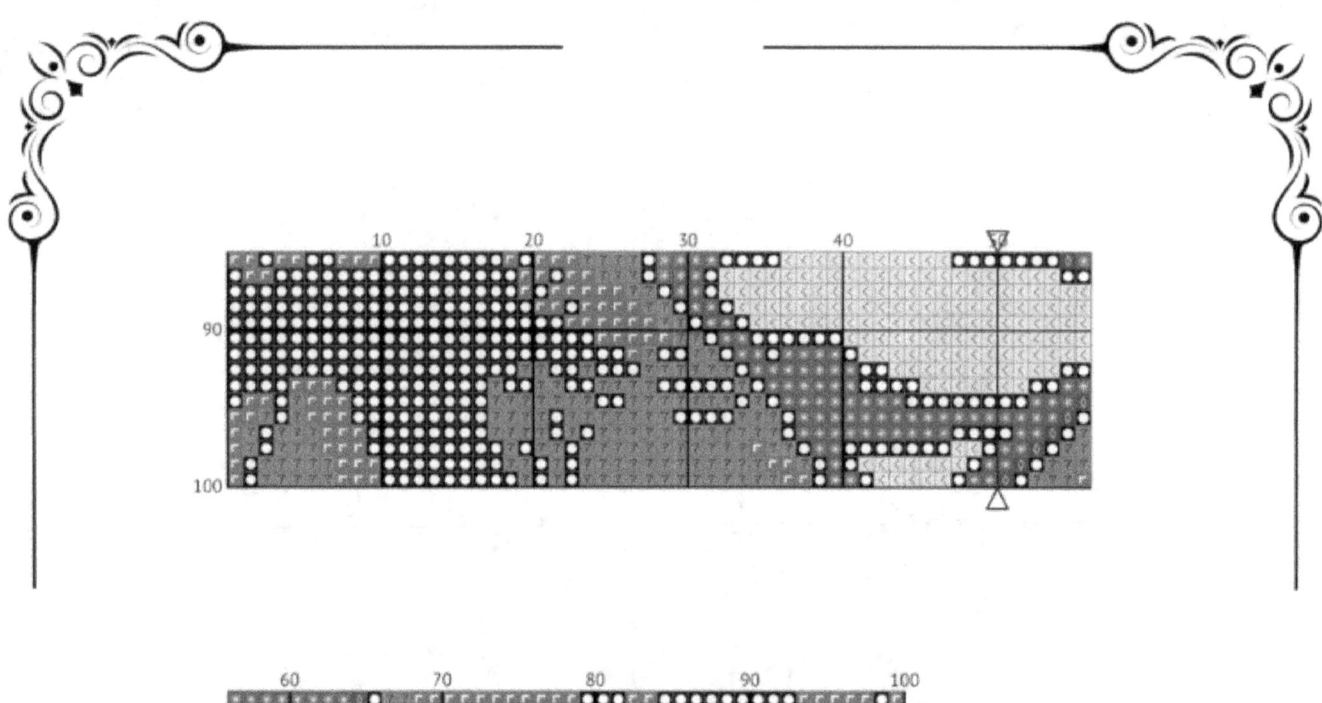

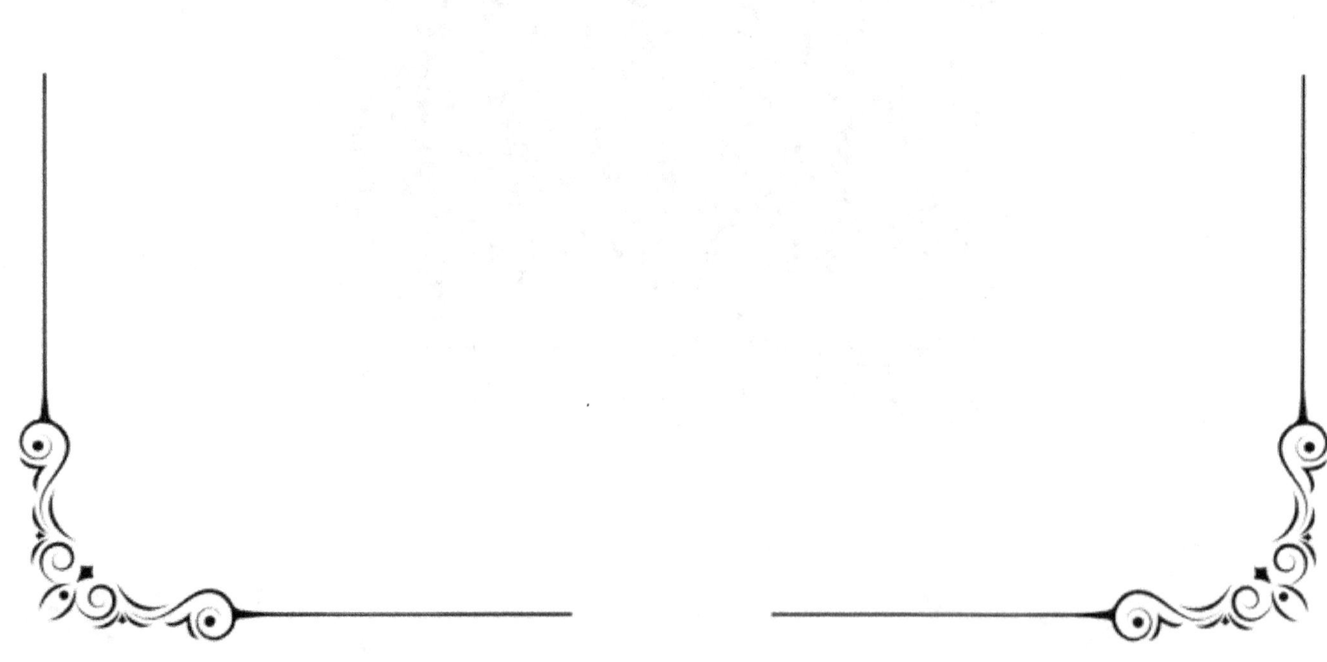

Design size: 120 x 180 stitches

Floss list for crosses

Use 2 strands of thread for cross stitch

N	Symbol		Number	Name	Stitches
1	T	T	DMC B5200	Snow White	333
2	<	<	DMC 310	Black	6458
3	7	7	DMC 349	Coral - Dark	2948
4	S	S	DMC 452	Shell Gray - Medium	272
5	✳	✳	DMC 645	Beaver Gray - Very Dark	3325
6	>	>	DMC 3779	Rosewood - Very Light	888

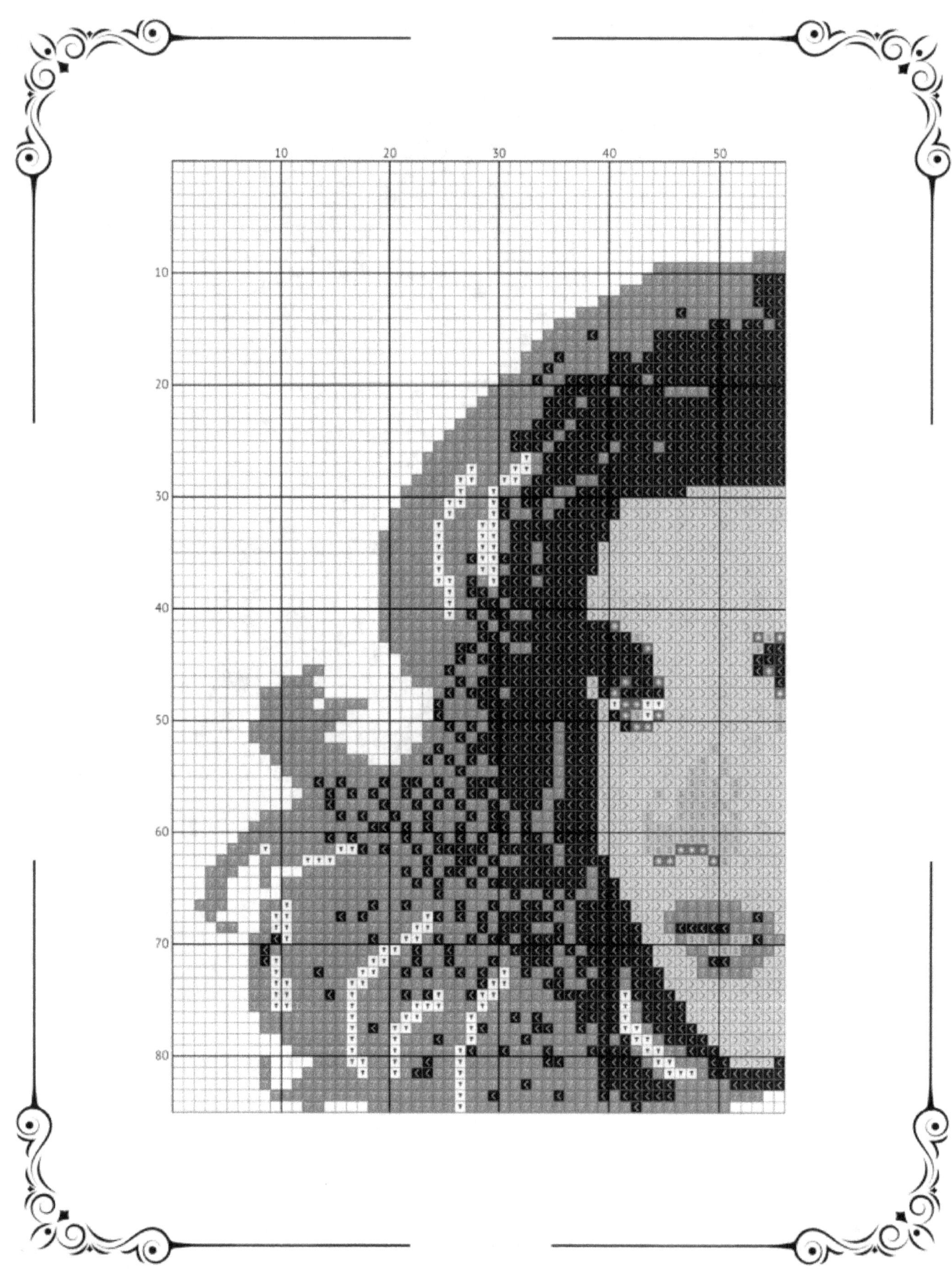

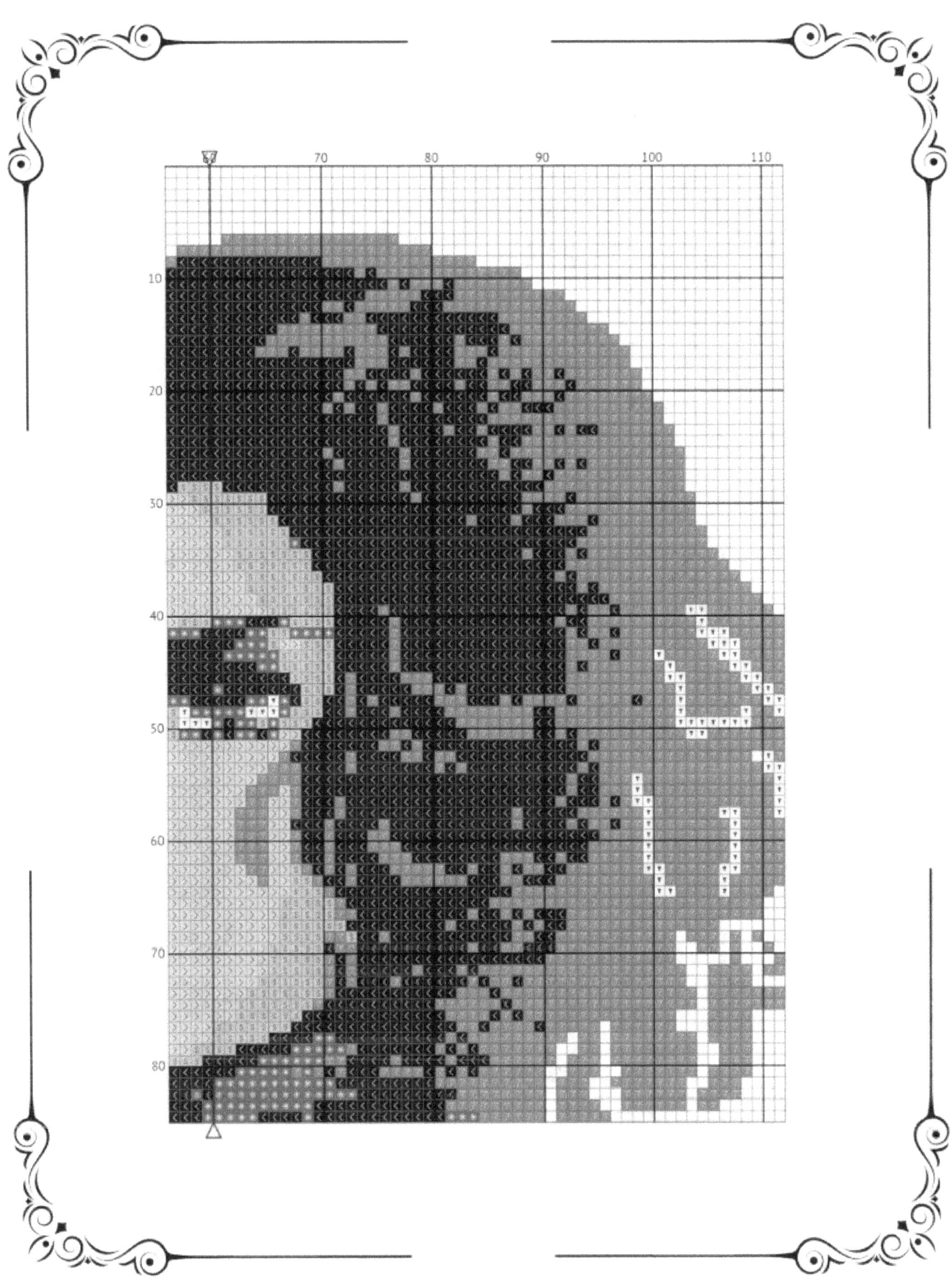

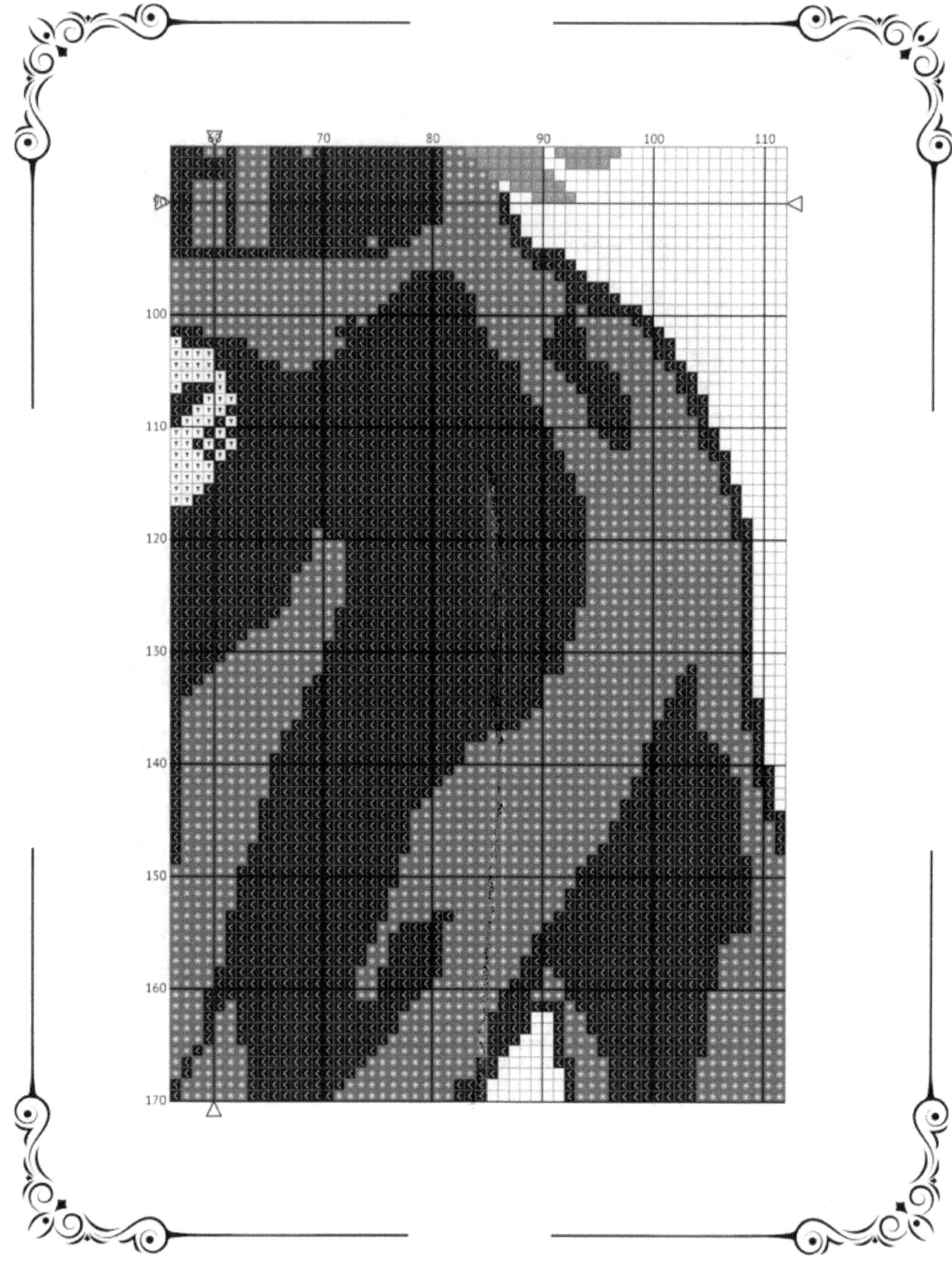

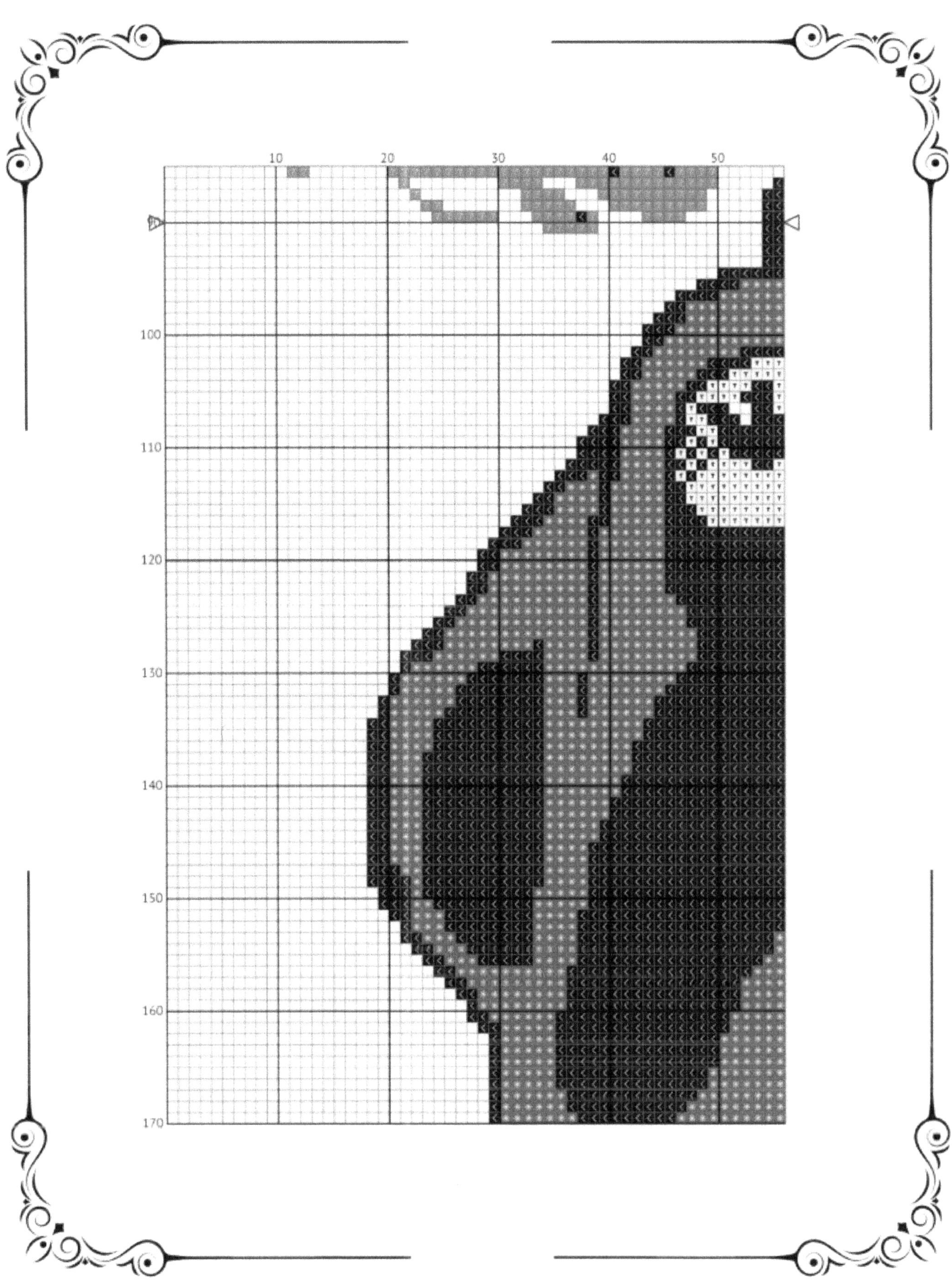

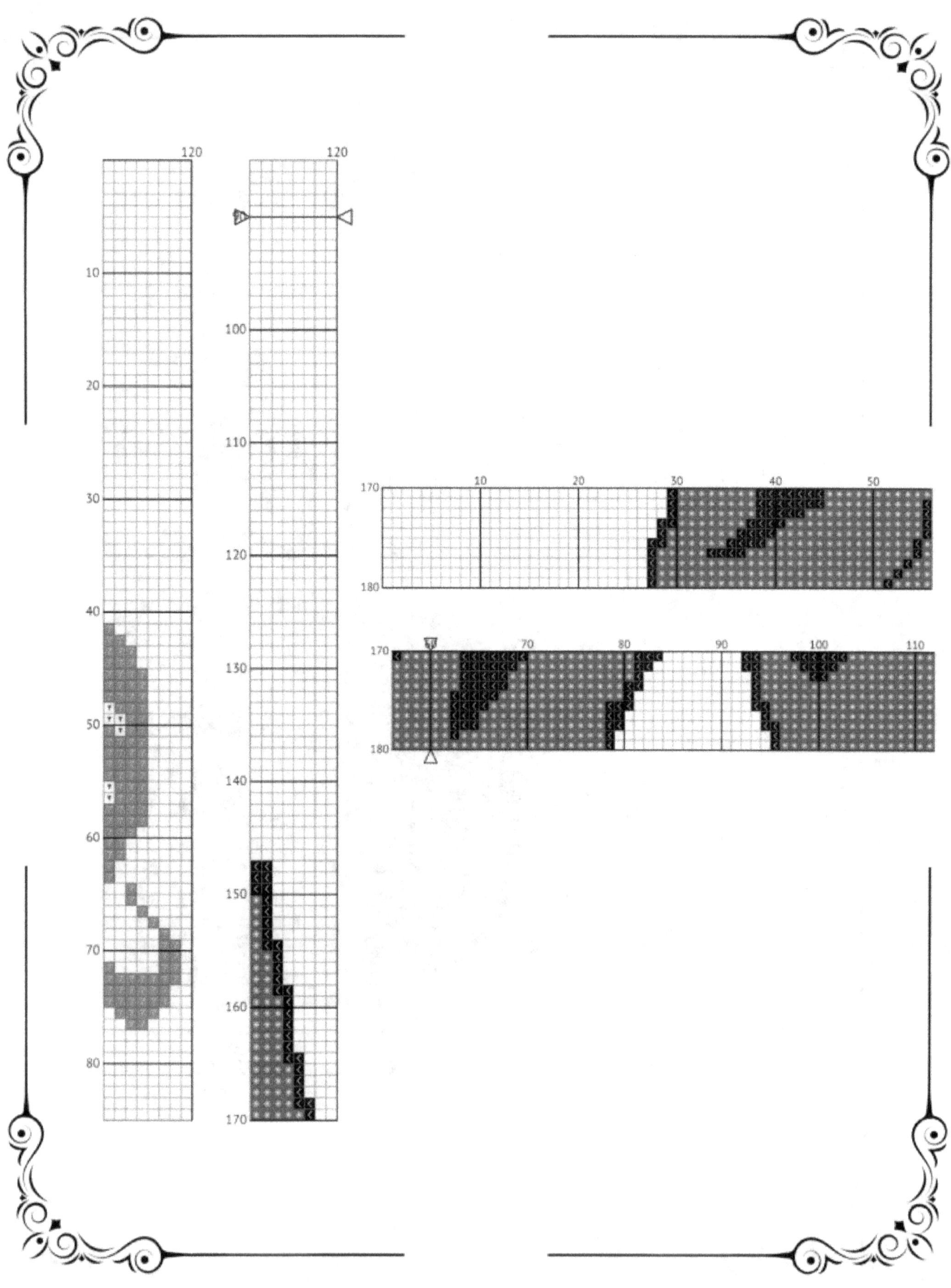

Design size: 111 x 62 stitches

Floss list for crosses

Use 2 strands of thread for cross stitch

N	Symbol		Number	Name	Stitches
1	✕	✕	DMC B5200	Snow White	84
2	◺	◺	DMC 18	Yellow Plum	349
3	m	m	DMC 22	Alizarin	86
4	◢	◢	DMC 310	Black	1257
5	●	●	DMC 451	Shell Gray - Dark	250
6	◊	◊	DMC 518	Wedgwood - Light	75
7	♡	♡	DMC 680	Old Gold - Dark	294
8	≡	≡	DMC 775	Baby Blue - Very Light	94
9	○	○	DMC 900	Burnt Orange - Dark	65
10	☆	☆	DMC 930	Antique Blue - Dark	259
11	♣	♣	DMC 945	Tawny	1246
12	▽	▽	DMC 3864	Mocha Beige - Light	297

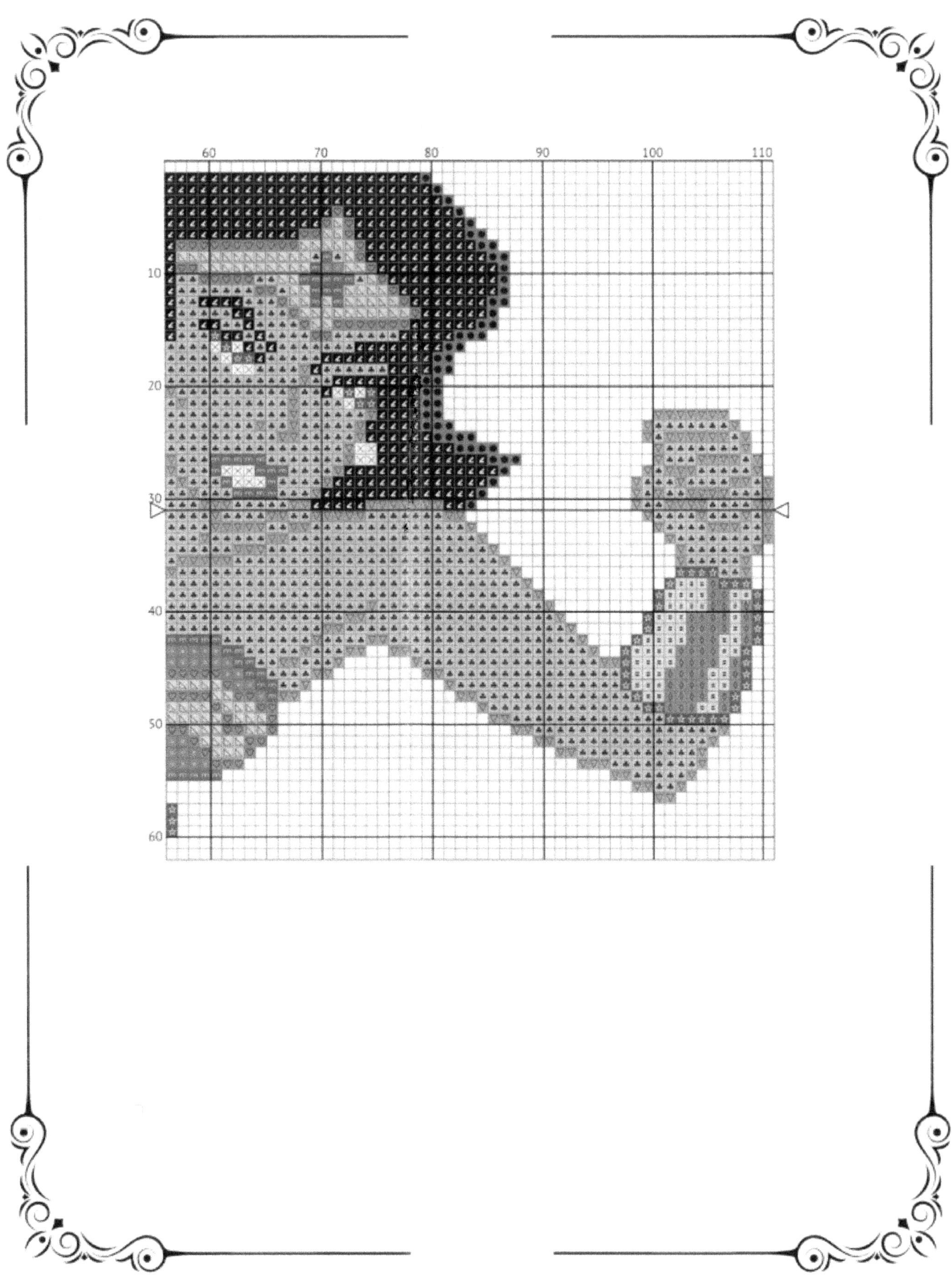

Design size: 46 x 57 stitches

Floss list for crosses

Use 2 strands of thread for cross stitch

N	Symbol		Number	Name	Stitches
1	◢	◢	DMC B5200	Snow White	178
2	●	◻	DMC 310	Black	1424

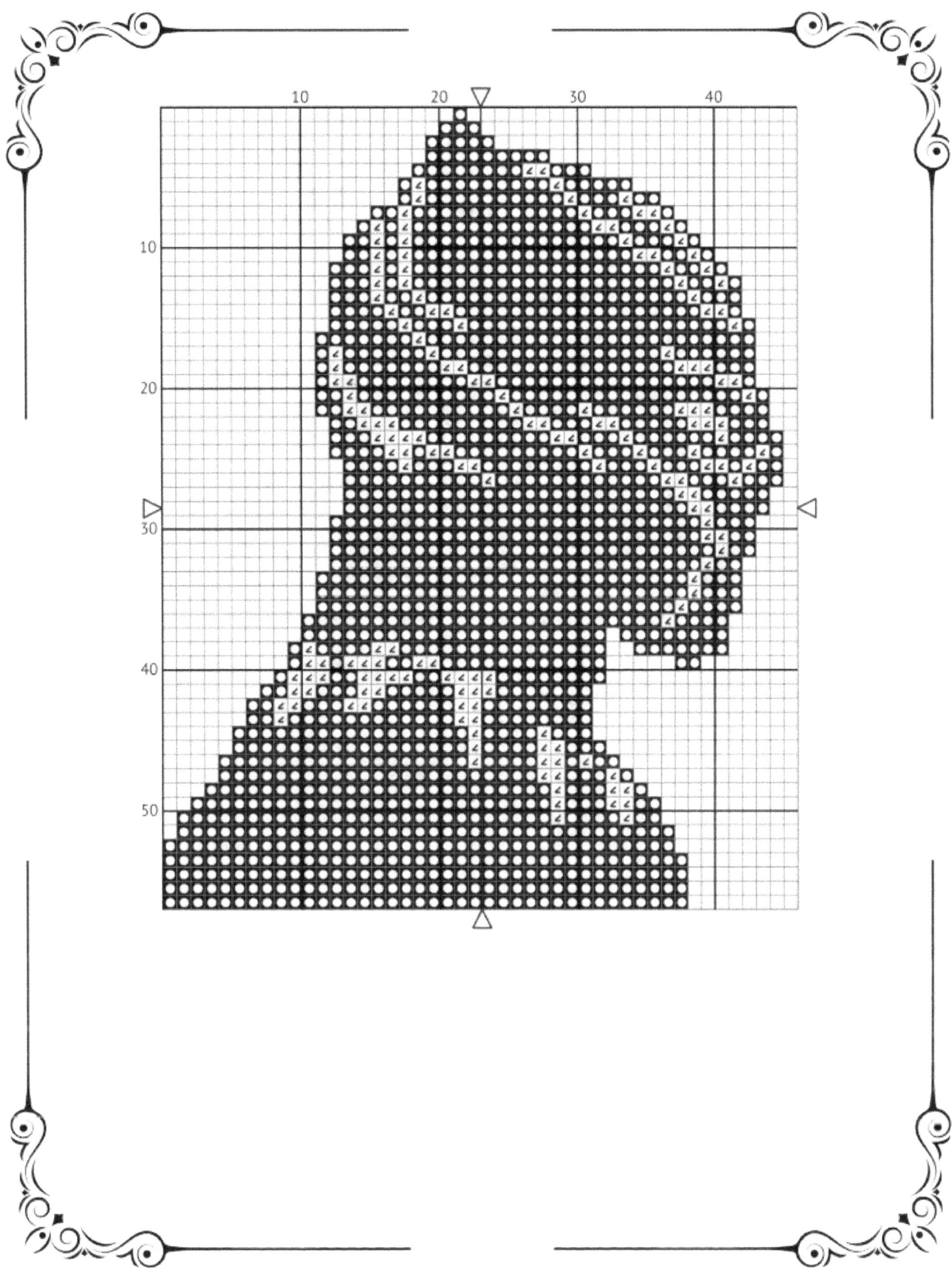

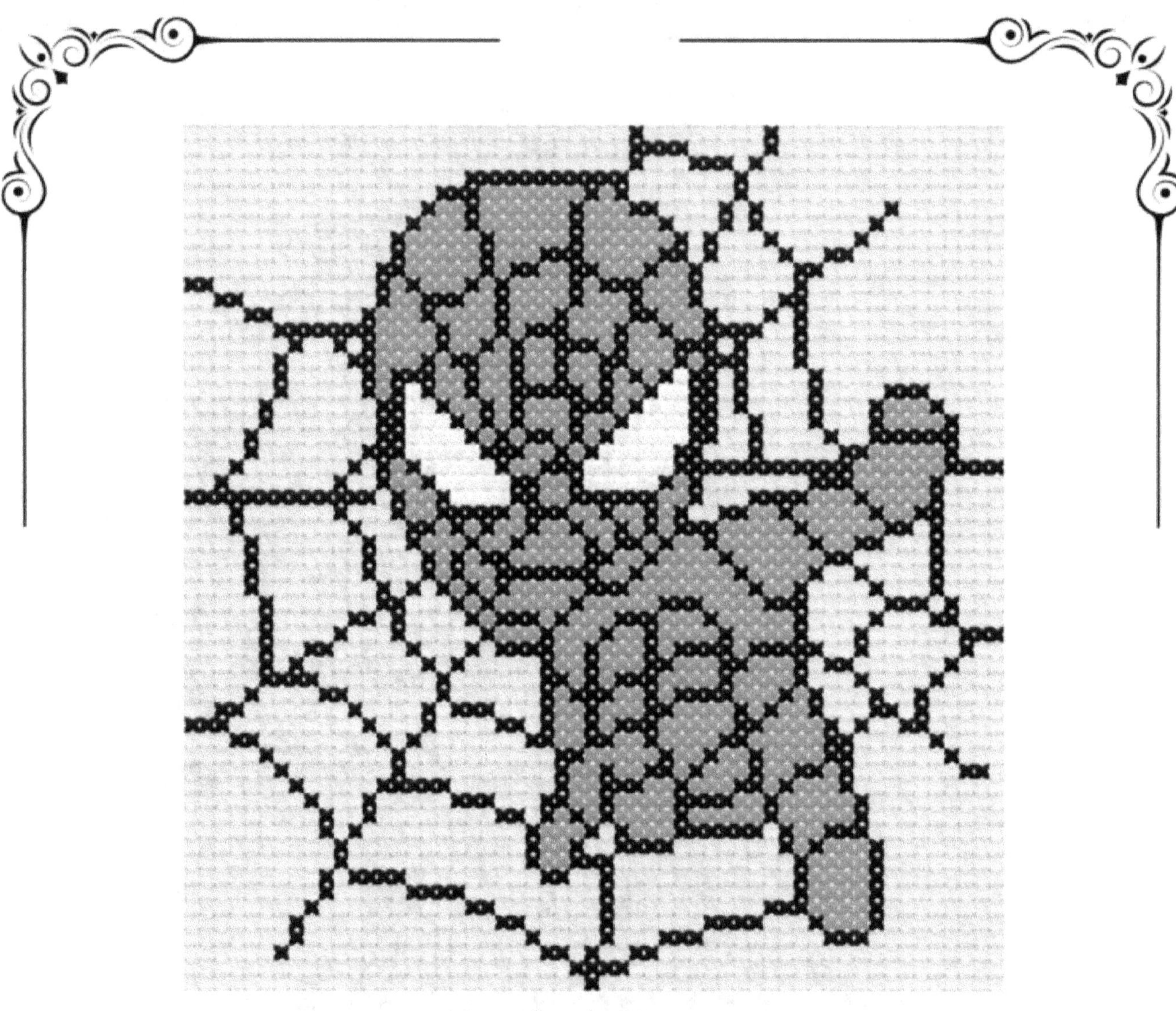

Design size: 55 x 57 stitches

Floss list for crosses

Use 2 strands of thread for cross stitch

N	Symbol		Number	Name	Stitches
1	♡	♡	DMC B5200	Snow White	59
2	●	◨	DMC 310	Black	729
3	∠	∠	DMC 946	Burnt Orange - Medium	570

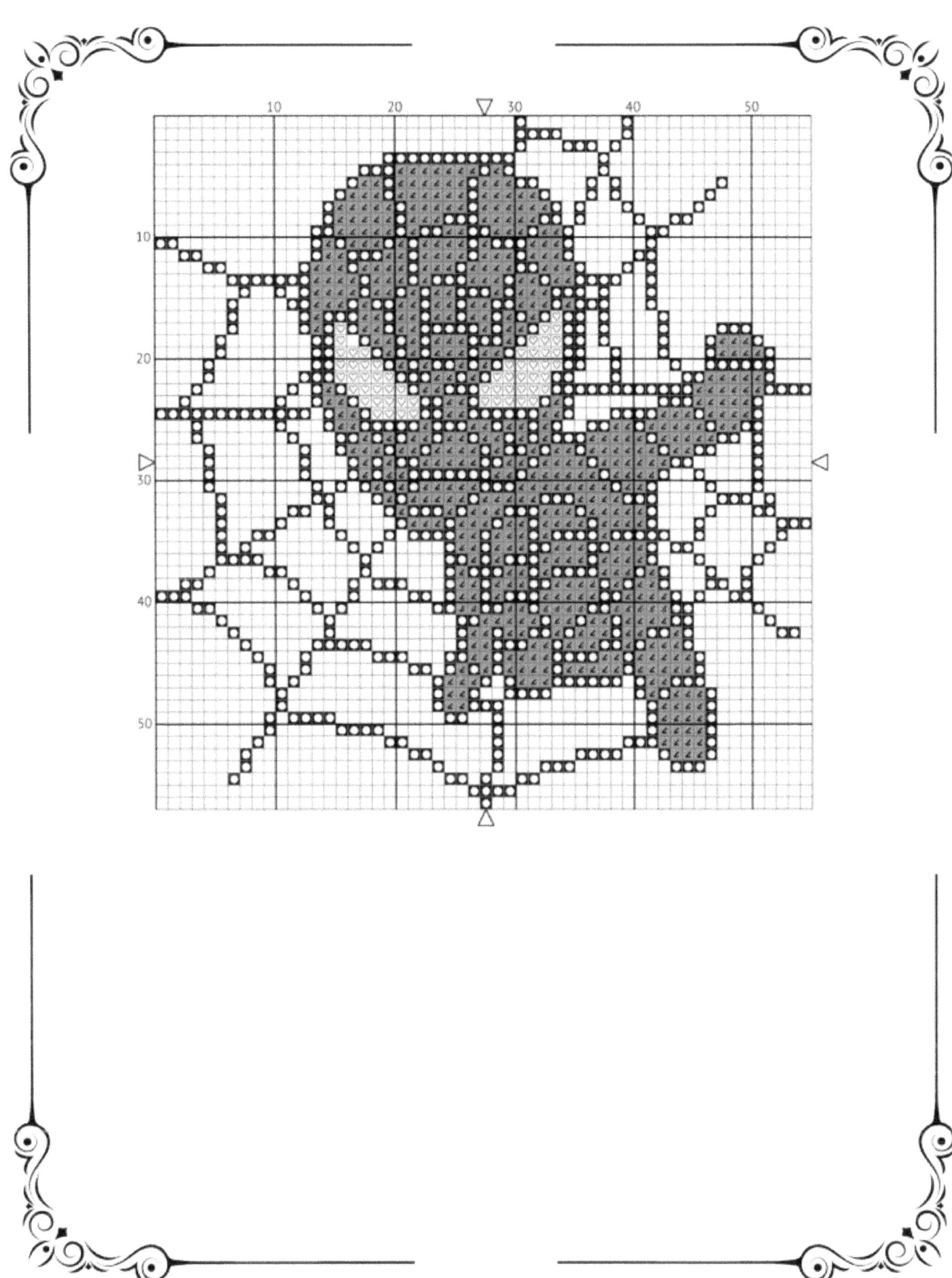